What other leaders say about *People Skills 3.0: Leadership Skills for Project Success:*

"Excellent leadership, in *any* setting, at *any* level, requires excellent interpersonal skills. *People Skills 3.0* excels in presenting these skills in practical and tangible ways that allow you to immediately apply them in your project or program work."

> **Tom Johnson, former president of CNN**, publisher of the *Los Angeles Times*, a White House Fellow, and Chairman Emeritus of the Lyndon Baines Johnson Foundation Board of Trustees

"Steve Flannes has a unique ability to identify and describe the people skills required for project leadership success. In this book, he offers a clear path to leadership success for next-generation project leaders. His ideas are innovative, and are also grounded in the realities of projectized work."

> **Ginger Levin, PMP, PgMP, OPM 3 Certified,** consultant, educator, author (*Program Management: A Life Cycle Approach*), and the 2014 recipient of the Project Management Institute's "Eric Jenett Project Management Excellence Award"

"Being a project leader in the 21st century requires interpersonal flexibility and comfort with ambiguity and the unknown. In this refreshing approach to increasing your ability to embrace paradox and grow your interpersonal skills, Dr. Flannes covers important topics, such as reframing, tracking, making manifest, and a collection of other techniques that will help you master being a next-generation project leader."

> **Cynthia Snyder Dionisio, PMP, MBA**, chair, PMBOK Guide (sixth edition), consultant, author (*PMP Certification All-in-One for Dummies*), and educator (University of Washington, California Institute of Technology). She served as the project manager for the 2008 editions of the *PMBOK(R) Guide* and the *Standards for Program Management*

"People don't work together—they LIVE together, and it's our relationships that make the difference between success and disaster in the workplace. Buy this book and keep it handy in your office. Makes your "personal best" happen by *building on what you have* and letting you know where to shift and focus—rather than trying to learn a new paradigm that might get quickly dated."

> **Jean Pare, M.Sc.** (London School of Economics), Director, Urban Mobility Solutions, Xerox: Québec, Canada

"The mindfulness approach described by Mike Mombrea (Chapter 9) is a powerful remedy for turning lives around. The tangible application of mindfulness practices to address the demands of a 24/7 work world are invaluable. I highly recommend this book!"

Adeline Johnson, Adeline Mortgage Team

"We live in a complex world where the element of unknown increases drastically every day, and in order to deliver successful projects and programs, we need to learn how to best deal with it. We also need an ability to think broad and act small, work with multiple cultures and yet maintain a personal approach.... Additionally, we face multitasking, and need the ability to stay focused.... I think Steve did a fantastic job covering all those topics in the greatest detail in his book, and he is best suited to address these topics given his broad experience and background."

Anna Hakobyan, PMP, Client Partner, Bertelsman-Arvato Systems (business systems design), North America (New York)

PEOPLE SKILLS 3.0:
NEXT-GENERATION LEADERSHIP SKILLS
FOR PROJECT SUCCESS

Steven Flannes, Ph.D.

People Skills Publishing
Piedmont, CA

ISBN-13: 978-0692374610 (People Skills Publishing)

ISBN-10: 0692374612

Dedication

To the unique people in our lives who influence our growth in the best of ways, by supporting our strengths while also gently nudging us towards changes that enable our possibilities.

Acknowledgments

My family, and especially my wife, Ann, have been very supportive and patient regarding all the time I have spent putting this book together, and deserve endless thanks and appreciation.

As I mention in the *Preface*, Dr. Ginger Levin has played a big role for me over the years in the exploration and refinement of these types of ideas, as well as being very supportive of my general focus on the people skills component of leadership.

Larry Butler, MA, in many diverse settings, has offered incisive thoughts and observations about the "people skills" intricacies of leadership.

In addition to authoring Chapter 11, Jonathan Flannes edited many of the other chapters, adding a fresh eye (especially to those chapters dealing with any aspect of positive psychology), reflective of his being a member of that next generation of leaders for whom this book is devoted.

Stephen Miller, MA, my lifelong friend, offered a supportive and meaningful review of various sections of the manuscript, applying his expertise as an educator to the construction of the ideas, as well as the writing style and presentation format.

Kathleen Kline's editorial skills (www.kathleenkline.com) took a ragged manuscript and applied clarity, discipline, and structure to its final shape and appearance. Additionally, she provided wise counsel on both the benefits and perils of self-publication.

A book of this reflective nature is ultimately the product of my experiential learnings derived from a lifetime of interpersonal interactions, such as working with individuals and also with small groups. All of the people who have attended my people skills seminars over the years deserve my thanks, both for their willingness to be active participants in the seminars, as well as for their probing questions and the personal observations they shared. Such input has helped me personally learn more about both my strengths and my weaknesses as a leader.

Preface

Why *This* Book?

I wrote this book because I believe that the interpersonal aspects of leadership constitute the most important professional (and often overlooked) competencies for the project professional.

- I believe this is a unique view of leadership in contrast to more traditional apvproaches that minimize the interpersonal dynamics that impact individual and organizational performance
- This is *not* your standard book on project leadership

This book presents you with practical leadership skills that are often not talked about or identified. These skills will help you:

- Improve your success as a project, program, portfolio, or functional leader
- Increase your success in our complex, multinational marketplace
- Expand your enjoyment and your level of satisfaction in your work
- Reduce work-related stress
- Increase your career options, making you more valuable as enterprise models continue to evolve, and as your professional and personal priorities change over your career

I want to make one key point before going any further:

This book is a collection of important lessons I have learned in my unique career as:

- A clinical psychologist
- An operations leader, and
- A project professional

From these three worlds, I share with you what I have learned about the interpersonal skills needed for leadership. These lessons surface from both my failures and my successes, but mostly from my failures.

More Benefits for You

This book provides you with two major, distinct benefits:

1. Descriptions of the **emerging leadership challenges** facing you, the enterprise professional
2. **Innovative yet tangible skills** that you can apply to master these leadership challenges

Together, these two benefits help you "thrive," and not just "survive" in your work.

And always remember:

- You may be a designated manager or leader, or you may be a team member with no formal leadership title
- Regardless, you need to have finely-honed leadership skills, because absolutely *nothing* gets done in the matrix system of projectized work without your ability to "lead" assorted stakeholders towards task completion

My Journey So Far

As I mentioned, this book is the result of my background as an operations leader, a clinical psychologist, and my experience in project management. I believe my background allows me to present creative and innovative ideas about how you can develop leadership skills, and thoughts on how you can then employ these sophisticated but tangible skills to increase your robustness as a leader.

I went to graduate school to become a clinical psychologist, due to my interest in considering how people and systems function, and to be of service in helping others make changes.

Early in my career, I worked in a variety of clinical settings (from hospitals to clinics), where I had the chance to witness people going through both the best and the worst of the human experience. In those settings, I saw how people pulled themselves out of personally dark places, identified the skills they needed to succeed in their respective environments, and then took the required concrete steps to make changes to increase their interpersonal skill sets.

After a number of years in direct clinical work, I served in a variety of operations and management positions where I directed service delivery functions, helped develop operations teams within an entrepreneurial setting, and managed teams and projects in health care and consulting.

My work in articulating these interpersonal leadership components of project teams began with a presentation I made to the Project Management Institute (PMI) Symposium in Long Beach, California, in 1998.

My presentation, which used a model of individual differences to leverage the personal styles of team members to obtain optimal team performance, received a very good response (At that time, there was a developing interest in the people side of project management).

The positive reaction to my work, plus the profession's increasing awareness of the need for more attention to people and leadership issues, resulted in my collaborating with Dr. Ginger Levin, PMP, PgMP, and OPM3 Certified, on the books *People Skills for Project Managers* (2000) and *Essential People Skills for Project Managers* (2005). Our first effort was translated into Russian, while the second book was translated into Japanese.

A Unique Team

Dr. Levin and I were indeed a unique team, she bringing an extensive career in both government and the private sector as a senior level project professional, author, and subject matter expert. For myself, I brought my experience as a psychologist who worked in leadership and project roles within a number of industries.

Together, we took pride in articulating tangible and practical leadership skills for the demanding and often nasty people issues in leading project teams. (Interestingly, we worked virtually on our books, never meeting in person until we conducted a PMI seminar in Seattle, WA, memorably on September 11, 2001).

This book owes much to the contributions of Dr. Levin, as well as the knowledge, input, and perspectives that I have acquired from working with project professionals in the United States and Canada, as well as England, Poland, and Ukraine. Additionally, I have learned much about the interpersonal side of leadership from my friend and colleague, Larry Butler, MA, with whom I have presented "people skills" seminars in many global locations.

What I Have Learned So Far

Throughout my career, I have continually been reminded of my three core beliefs:

1. The interpersonal skills of leadership are crucial and are always increasing in importance

2. I know that these skills can be clearly defined, practiced, and successfully implemented

3. I know that small improvements in these skills bring disproportionately big dividends in both individual leadership performance and team success

In essence, you do not need to be a natural "people person" to still be a very good project leader.

However, you do need to actively apply yourself to developing the leadership skills required in our continually emerging project world.

This book is your guide for your journey towards enhanced leadership development.

While these skills will help you be a more effective leader, they will also assist you in feeling less stress and frustration in your work, and will aid you in experiencing more effectiveness and enjoyment in your personal life.

What This Book Offers You

I describe current and future people-based leadership complexities you will face, and then I provide you with developmental solutions that you can follow to increase the skills needed to meet these leadership challenges.

Specifically, the book presents:

- **Next generational leadership challenges**, and what you as a leader should expect to see in our multicultural world of complexity and rapid change **(Chapter 1)**

- **The importance for you as a leader of "knowing yourself,"** because such self-knowledge serves as the foundation for you in using your personal essence towards developing sophisticated emotional intelligence, a key ingredient of the next generation leader **(Chapter 2)**

- **Guidelines for how you can make the personal changes that you will need to make** to stay current and potent as a leader. Leaders with the ability to fluidly continue to re-define themselves over time will flourish; others will fail **(Chapter 3)**

- **What are the personal attributes**, skills, and qualities that the successful global leader needs, and how can you develop your own plan towards achieving and expanding these skills? **(Chapter 4)**

- **What are the distinct leadership competencies that you will need to lead** successful project teams in our world noted for economic, cultural, and technological complexity? **(Chapter 5)**

- **What are unique approaches you can follow to achieve high levels of performance**, and how can you return to those high performance levels even after you or your team have experienced an intense, negative event or crisis experience? **(Chapter 6)**

- What can you do as a leader to **create and nurture the very best team culture**, one noted for creativity, effective interpersonal functioning, and high achievement? **(Chapter 7)**

- What are distinct and sophisticated approaches you can apply to **manage the negative influence of inevitable conflict**, and keep the team moving forward towards goal completion? **(Chapter 8)**

- How can you apply concrete and tangible approaches from the worlds of **neuroscience and mindfulness** to function at your highest levels of performance while still maintain balance in your life? **(Mike Mombrea, Chapter 9)**

- Discover **the leadership lessons from a senior level leader** who has worked in many demanding settings, as well as seeing what 43 other extremely successful leaders said are the key leadership attributes that they have noticed over their careers. **(Larry Butler, Chapter 10)**

- How is **positive psychology** viewed by a member of the **next generation of leaders**? In this chapter, a member of this next generation shares his observations about how positive psychology behaviors, demonstrated by leaders in different industries, have increased their effectiveness in leading teams **(Jonathan Flannes, Chapter 11)**

- What **future global challenges** will you face you as a leader, and what are some innovative approaches you can take to identify the presence of these forces and prepare yourself to continue to be "the evolving people-centric leader?" **(Chapter 12)**

*   *   *   *   *

When I think about what I have learned in my leadership career, and then reflect upon what I hear from others who also lead teams and projects, I come away firmly believing the following:

As leader, you can easily learn to address the technical challenges you face.

1. The people issues of leadership, however, are the most challenging, but they will offer you the greatest professional and personal rewards.

This book is your practical companion as you face and conquer the emerging interpersonal leadership demands of our global and rapidly evolving economy.

In today's world of a multinational economy and projectized work settings, we all are "leaders" in our respective enterprise efforts, regardless of whether or not we formally hold that title. I hope this book adds both value and enjoyment to your experience as leader.

Steven Flannes
Piedmont, California
January 2015

stevenflannes@att.net

Table of Contents

Chapter 1
Next Generation Leadership Challenges:
What's Coming Your Way?

Steven Flannes

Project leadership is a complicated process, requiring a breadth of both technical skills and people skills. As you know, the people challenges in project leadership can be messy, nasty, uncomfortable, and extremely frustrating.

Additionally, these leadership challenges are made even more complicated by the presence of rapid global economic changes, as well as the emergence of radical ways of perceiving how teams function within the complex milieu of melding cultures and economies.

As organizations have become more global and cross-cultural, a shift in leadership style has occurred—a shift requiring sophisticated people skills. This management style, exemplified by the influenced-based project leader, is consensual and participative, calling for the leader to be adept in many roles and skills.

What Are the Emerging Trends?

In this chapter, I want to offer a succinct overview of emerging trends and forces that I believe create the requirement for interpersonally sophisticated leadership skills.

I will not attempt to offer an extensive or complete overview of such forces, as such depth is not appropriate for the goals of this book. Rather, I will present certain trends and forces that have caught my eye in recent years, developments that I believe hold great significance for you, the leader.

(*Note*: Throughout this book, I use the term project "leader" to apply to all project professionals, because you need to "lead" in your project tasks even if you do not have the formal title of project "leader").

Contemporary Leadership Challenges

You face challenges in leading teams to project success due to three contemporary forces. These three distinct but overlapping forces are:

- The existence of core aspects of project management that are inherently challenging
- Global social and political trends impacting commerce
- Emerging new frameworks for looking at how organizations operate

Leadership Challenges Related to Core Project Processes

The core aspects of projectized work milieus contain a number of attributes that I believe increase your leadership challenges.

The first of these complicating variables is the fact that projects are really technical problems driven by human complexities. While this point is widely accepted, it often does not get enough attention, in my view, when considering the variables influencing a successful project.

Too often, process methodologies can falsely suggest that the project processes and stages emerge in a nicely evolving linear manner, mirroring the initial scope. In reality, leaders are wise to perceive project progression as not a linear process.

Secondly, project leadership positions are made more difficult by the increase in project complexity, plus the fact that team members often experience divided loyalties, as they may be working simultaneously on a number of separate projects.

The final variable impacting leadership ease is the presence of new project technologies or process, as evidence by the emersion of Agile approaches to project completion.

Economic Trends Impacting Enterprise Leadership

The emergence of the global economy has led to a brisk pace of enterprise chaos and change, followed by institutional consolidation. This brisk pace of change is seen on societal levels such as the rapid upheavals in the Middle East, where long-term citizen dissatisfaction spawns movements noted for initial chaos and disruption, followed by a reconsolidation of power and institutional functioning.

This process of the economic chaos-and-reintegration evolution is often viewed as a necessary evil, reminiscent of Schumpeter's economic theory of "creative destruction." (Flannes, M., 2011). And in a world where instability is present, and where creative destruction is viewed as an apt description of current enterprise and societal change patterns, then you as project leader are faced with huge challenges in finding ways to lead during these turbulent times.

Substantial Growth in Regional Economies

The regional economies of the world are growing at remarkable rates, creating enterprise opportunities in emerging countries heretofore not on the world economic radar screen. The growth of such economies requires that project leaders develop cultural competency in geographical regions where many project leaders have not worked, or even visited.

Take a look at Table 1.1 below, which illustrates the countries with the fastest growing gross national products.

Quite a varied list of countries, probably countries in which many of us have not visited. Thus, the next generation project leader, working within such diverse countries and cultures, will certainly need a variety of leadership skills to meld individuals into teams.

Table 1.1

Top Ten Countries in 2013 with the Highest Percentage Growth in Real GNP

(Source: *The CIA World Fact Book- 2013*)

Country	Real GNP % Growth Rate
1. South Sudan	24.70
2. Sierra Leone	13.30
3. Turkmenistan	12.20
4. Paraguay	12.06
5. Macau	11.90
6. Mongolia	11.80
7. Turks and Caicos	11.20
8. Moldova	8.90
9. Laos	8.30
10. Timor-Leste	8.10

Obviously, this list suggests a huge variety in both cultures and locations. As you look at the list, ask yourself how you would fare in leading a team composed of team members from those countries and cultures. To me, the list suggests that you will need to be a leader adept in interpersonal flexibility as well as a basic comfort in dealing with ambiguity and the unknown.

Emerging Depth Models
of Organizational-Systems Operation

A spectrum of writers, researchers, and philosophers, representing a breadth of intellectual and innovative perspectives, is starting to describe economic-systemic forces and concepts that heretofore have remained insulated within academic settings. These models and perspectives shine light on the powerful forces that you contend with when you are leading a team in today's world.

Each of these innovative models of the world, and the concomitant functioning of organizations and systems, suggest that it's a much more complicated, fluid, and unpredictable world out there than we would often like to believe.

And assuming that such complexity, fluidity, and unpredictability do exist, then next generation leaders need to be aware of these forces. Additionally, next generation leaders will need to ramp up their skills in embracing these forces, and in leading teams under such conditions.

These innovative forces and models of organization are described below, and include applications from complexity theory and from "design thinking."

Complexity Theory and Leadership

As I view complexity theory, projects and programs do not adhere to the linear, logical rules of self-organization and progression often ascribed to a PMBOK mindset of stages and processes. Consequently, complexity theory suggests that as the leader, you should not over-emphasize long-term planning and risk management at the expense of losing focus on the importance of being able to manage the following variables:

- Embracing the lack of predictability

- Functioning while acknowledging paradox

- Mediating subgroup conflict as well as rigid beliefs

This application of complexity thinking to project leadership is seen in greater detail, I believe, in the work of Stacey (1996), who describes principles that serve as a foundation for a complexity-based view of organizations, and in my view, of teams.

Some of Stacey's work (modified here for the application to teams) that I think can be nicely applied to the complexity of projectized work include, in part, the ideas that:

- Groups are composed of non-linear feedback systems, that operate in stable ways, but also in unstable ways

- This interplay between stability and instability is both natural and desired, as the oscillation between those states can result in innovation. Consider the following two implications for teams and systems: Too much "stability" creates a difficulty for making change. Too much instability results in chaos or disintegration

In my view, these principles imply that you the leader need to find comfort with the idea that project teams operate much more in non-linear manners than we often assume. And as a result, you need to have a sophisticated and robust interpersonal skill set to comfortably succeed in such complex systems.

When I consider complexity theory, I also come away believing that you as leader need to find ways to successfully keep your team functioning at the intersection of routine (represented by your procedures and operational guidelines) and minimal structure (represented by your ability to allow team members to pursue idiosyncratic paths towards the goal of innovation).

Achieving and maintaining the balance of this intersection, within your team, is an art form. This balance is best achieved when you the leader are cognitively and interpersonally flexible, as well as being confident in trusting in the basic process of group achievement. Thus, the leader achieves a quality product by:

- Using available resources (both technical and interpersonal)

- Successfully embracing program influences (both positive and negative)

- Knowing how and when to let team members follow idiosyncratic paths and how and when to exert team structure

Using Design Thinking in Leadership

Another interesting model that I believe offers a powerful way of looking at systems, teams, and organizations is the concept of "design thinking." This way of viewing systems suggests that the leader should lead from a posture grounded in an integration of the best aspects of two divergent approaches (Brown, 2009).

These two approaches to viewing optimal organizational functioning consist of one approach that is, in my words, people-centric (looking at the variables of intuition, feeling and inspiration) and one approach that is rational-analytic (looking at objective measures such as market viability and product quality).

Brown, writing on an implication of design thinking, encourages leaders to embrace three distinct aspects of business operation. These aspects include:

- The human factor (i.e., what people want in a new product)

- The technical aspect (how feasible is the desired product?)

- The business aspect (is the product viable in the marketplace?)

Such an approach clearly is not linear in nature, and requires leaders who can comfortably shift their focus back and forth among the three distinct aspects of business operations.

The Resulting New Generation Leadership Skills

I have just presented thoughts on some of the trends and forces that I believe create your need for sophisticated interpersonal leadership skills.

These forces, as mentioned, include the core dimensions of projectized work that make it a difficult way to work, the rapid economic growth of previously low-profile regional economies, the leadership skills required within the framework of complexity theory, and the interpersonal leadership demands inherent in the innovative business approaches such as design thinking.

Research on distinctive leadership skills is also identifying specific skills that you will need to have in order to lead. Presented below is a sampling of some of the current work on describing leadership skills that I believe you need for next generation leadership.

What Are These Leadership Skills?

A number of authors are commenting on these increasingly sophisticated skills that project leaders will need to address the people component of enterprise success.

Gerush and West (2009), for example, looking at trends in IT project leadership, note that "soft skills are as important as understanding processes and practices."

Specifically, Gerush and West identify ten core competencies for next generation project leadership, and six of these competencies directly related to the leader's interpersonal skills. These core competencies include, in part, an awareness of different types of communication, the ability to adapt communication to the current setting, and a competency that is gaining popularity—that being the concept of "servant" leadership.

In an article that describes similar attributes needed for the people-effective leader of projects, Suhonen and Paasivaara (2011) speak to the importance of the presence of "human capital"" in successful projects. In this case, human capital involves attributes such as trust, commitment, team culture, and the emotional intelligence of the project manager.

Gerush and West, along with Suhonen and Paasivaara, thus identify a depth of skill in the people aspect of project leadership that often is not considered in the project management literature. Indeed, when I review the professional standards (PMBOK) of the Project Management Institute (PMI, 2008), I see the need for leadership skills, but the treatment and description of such skills appear to me to be more general, and less operational.

These sophisticated leadership skills (needed in disparate political, social, and economic systems) are also being described in the literature as "global leadership skills."

For example, Holt and Seki (2012) offer a very complete and sophisticated treatment of the next generation's need for global leadership skills. In reviewing their work, one sees the importance that they place on the people skill component of global leadership competencies. They argue that traditional models of leadership have been too Western-centric, linear in nature, and lacking of an appreciation for leveraging multicultural differences for enterprise success.

Specifically, Holt and Seki suggest that next generation leaders need to have skills in:

- Multicultural effectiveness and a cosmopolitan attitude (a variation, to me, of the injunction to "act locally while thinking globally")

Boyacigller (2012) also speaks to the importance of global leadership in articulating a need for a "global mindset." This leadership mindset involves your acceptance of the value of multicultural realities, as well as your being able to adopt a positive attitude towards embracing cognitive complexity.

Where is This All Going?

The research and perspectives described in this chapter briefly capture the current and future needs for sophisticated leadership skills grounded in interpersonal abilities. These skills and abilities will bridge cultural divides.

Below is my own list of such skills and abilities. My work as a psychologist and a leader has resulted in my having an experientially-defined list of the mindsets and skills that you will need for next generation leadership success. Here is my list:

- Your willingness to maintain an open mindset as to what is "normal" and your ability to artfully grasp the norms and values of the stakeholders with whom you are working

- Your ability to quickly form productive interpersonal relationships through an interpersonal posture of being genuinely humble

- (Being humble, in my mind, involves your treating others with a fundamental respect, the absence of "putting on airs," and a willingness to view others as inherently equal)

- Embracing the belief that all stakeholders are your "teachers," and each offers you lessons and opportunities for your growth

- Your ability to be "present," attending to what is happening in the moment, plus the ability to really "see" what is taking place with people and projects

- Your ability to not just live with paradox, but to embrace it, as it is the path to project innovation, team achievement, as well as your own career enjoyment and personal development

Hopefully, I have provided a context for my view of the challenges facing next generation leaders. Having set the stage, I will now move along to describing the distinct interpersonal skills you need for leadership success.

The First Skill: Know Yourself

The first required skill I will address is your ability to "know yourself." Such knowledge serves as bedrock for all of your interpersonal leadership and people skills.

By adopting an ongoing focus on self-knowledge, you are creating an introspective posture that provides you with a window into looking at what is going on with you regarding your thoughts, feelings, beliefs, and behaviors.

Chapter 2
Knowing Yourself:
There's No Better Place to Start

Steven Flannes

As a leader, you must develop a keen self-awareness. For example, how do you describe your personality? Are you interpersonally adept at relating to others? What are your strengths and weaknesses, especially during demanding periods?

This chapter encourages you to look within yourself in an honest, creative, ongoing manner, to ultimately assess your interpersonal strengths and shortcomings. In this chapter, you are presented with a number of paths one can follow towards the goal of gaining such self-awareness.

Without attaining this introspective insight, your efforts to achieve the necessary leadership skills will inevitably fall short. No meaningful effort in improving your leadership skills can happen without first committing to an ongoing process of sober self-reflection.

In recent years, I have noticed an increased appreciation, within the project world, of the importance of knowledge of the self. This is not to say, however, that self-knowledge is consistently pursued throughout the project world, as many disregard its importance in favor of alternative approaches. Such attitudes, in my opinion, place too much emphasis on the technical support tools of project management.

Additionally, for those who minimize the importance of the interpersonal aspect of project management, there is often the belief that the leader must "manage" their team members.

Such a focus places too much responsibility for the success or failure of a project on the technical tools of project task tracking. In contrast, this book stresses the importance of a project leader working on his or her own interpersonal skills to achieve enterprise success.

Achieving Self-Knowledge

The act of "knowing yourself" is a tall order. Where do you start? How can you find the necessary means of achieving such a multifaceted task?

In this chapter, I present a number of selected systems I find to be both helpful and practical in addressing this goal of knowing yourself. These are my personal favorites, ones I have found to be highly effective in the development of project leaders.

To better understand these systems, think of them as "cameras," each with the ability to capture a detailed picture, a novel perspective, or a side of you previously unexplored. Ultimately, these images begin to accumulate for you, and finally create a robust picture of who you are as a person.

It is important not to take these systems, and the resulting images they provide, too literally or seriously. I encourage you to utilize these systems to provide yourself with feedback *about who you are currently*. It is important, however, to try to stay away from seeing yourself as a fixed object. You are constantly changing as a person, as we all are, and consequently, your efforts at "knowing who you are" should be fluid and ongoing.

In this chapter, I cover topics such as:

- Gaining an awareness of your personal "style"
- Knowledge of your current career values
- The role you prefer to play within a team
- A description of the "Big Five" personality factors
- Your views on human nature
- How your personal history can impact who you are today

Awareness of Your Personal Style

Without getting stuck in an endless search for the "true you," it is still important that you have a working knowledge of your personal style, or personality.

This sense of self can provide you with a reference point to use whilst interacting with others. Such a point of reference offers guidance by highlighting several key elements of your personality. These reference points include:

- Familiar interpersonal patterns you tend to display
- How you like to communicate
- Your preferred method of planning and implementing your day

The MBTI Model of Self

One personal style system that I have found meaningful to project professionals in a variety of global settings is the Myers-Briggs Type Indicator (MBTI). The MBTI is applicable to the world of projects as a whole, and has been described extensively (Flannes and Levin, 2005). In accordance with this chapter's goal of heightening your self-knowledge, I will briefly describe the core concepts of this useful system, and discuss how they can help you achieve this objective.

Upon completion of the MBTI assessment, you receive a four-letter style reflecting your preferences on the assessment's four aspects of functioning.

While we all have a variety of differing qualities within us, the most important information the MBTI offers is a detailing of the preferences that describe our *primary tendencies.*

Descriptions of the MBTI preferences are presented below. With the goal of "knowing yourself" in mind, select the four preferences you think best describe you as you read through the descriptions. How do I get energized?

- **Extravert:** Gets energized from stimulation from others, or from the outside world
- **Introvert:** Is energized by more solitary or reflective activities or settings

How do I take in *new information*?

- **Sensing**: Desires to focus on tangible data, with a here-and-now time perspective

- **iNtuition**: Prefers to look at a situation from a big picture perspective, and with a future orientation

How do I prefer to *make decisions*?

- **Thinking**: Wants to use a logical or analytic approach to decision making

- **Feeling:** Prefers to focus on subjective considerations when making a decision

How do I like to *proceed* with a task?

- **Judging**: Strongly desires to plan the work, and then work the plan towards closure

- **Perceiving**: Wants to take a more casual and open-ended approach to routine and structure

Using the MBTI information presented above, you can quickly create a working description of your style in action. My MBTI style, for example, is "INFJ." Applying the above descriptions to my denoted style, my general functioning can be described as follow:

- I am energized by more solitary, reflective activities or settings *(Introversion)*

- I prefer to look at a situation from a big picture perspective *(iNtuition)*

- I tend to focus on subjective considerations when making a decision (*Feeling*)

- I have a strong desire to plan the work, and then work the plan until completion. *(Judging)*

So, if we were to take the above description of me—and apply it to "myself as project leader"—the following implications surface as challenges to my role as project leader:

- **Introversion**: I may not be sufficiently communicative with other stakeholders, often keeping too much to myself

- **iNtuition**: I will most likely enjoy the planning stage of a project, where "anything is possible." However, I might become bored or complacent during the documentation/completion stages

- **Feeling**: It is possible that I could focus too much on the soft aspects of the team, such as the group's morale and "mood," and neglect to be as task focused as is necessary

- **Judging**: Once a plan is conceived (i.e., the scope), I might be hesitant to change direction, even when presented with valid, relevant, or emerging new information (just ask my family for confirmation about this one!)

Now, you can see that this brief application of my MBTI style clearly offers some guidance regarding possible strengths and weaknesses I may bring to my role as project leader.

Clearly, much more could be emphasized here regarding the MBTI. For a wide range of MBTI products and publications, you can contact Consulting Psychologist Press (www.cpp-db.com) in the Americas, or OPP (www.opp.co) in the United Kingdom and Europe.

Knowledge of Your Current Career and Life Values

Another approach to better understanding yourself is an examination of the career-related values that often impact your choice of career function and direction.

One valuable, straightforward model for identifying such values is the innovative system developed by Edgar Schein. (Cullen and Christopher, 2012, and Flannes and Levin, 2005). His model describes one's individual motives, motivators, and values related to various work tasks.

Schein described these values as "career anchors." One's career anchors can be determined by completing a short self-assessment test. However, even if you do not complete the assessment, you can still find value in considering the concepts behind the eight anchors.

To understand these concepts, examine the 8 career anchors below, and choose the top 4 you find most appealing (these definitions reflect my modifications of the formal terms).

1. **Technical-Functional anchor**: For people who have this as a strong anchor, you want to do work that gives you the chance to feel that you are a subject matter expert in your particular field

2. **General Management anchor:** You desire to be in charge of a function, even if not formally the project manager

3. **Service anchor**: You desire to be of service to others, or to find yourself working for the greater good

4. **Entrepreneurial Creativity anchor**: You enjoy crafting the design of a product, and/or starting a business endeavor

5. **Autonomy anchor**: Even when working within a team, you desire to be self-directed and free to chart your own path

6. **Pure Challenge anchor**: You find excitement in attacking the toughest of challenges. Often, you find the challenge itself to be more important than the actual task at hand

7. **Security anchor**: You prefer continuity, stability, and predictability in work life (a rare experience in a projectized environment!)

8. **Lifestyle anchor:** A well-lived life is important to you, finding fulfillment in both work and personal environments. For some people, this is an example of the "work hard, play hard" mindset

As was done previously with the MBTI, let us now use my own career anchors as a way to illustrate how one's knowledge of their anchors can provide another vehicle for self-knowledge.

My four highest career anchors are as follows:

- Service

- Entrepreneurial Creativity

- Lifestyle

- Autonomy

Therefore, if I craft a narrative incorporating these four anchors, a resulting description of how I function might be as follows:

- I want to work with a great deal of freedom and self-direction (*Autonomy*)

- I want to be involved in start-up types of settings (*Entrepreneurial Creativity*) in which my product will be helpful to others *(Service)*

- While I acknowledge that the start-up milieu will require a great deal of hours, I nevertheless want to be able to periodically step away and pursue personal interests (*Lifestyle*). Consequently, I tend to define myself by my *avocations* as much as I do by my *vocation*

Thus, another picture of who I am emerges through the use of career anchors. Notice the following implications for me that this picture suggests regarding the position of project leader:

- I may not be very interested in managing the more structured aspects of the project (as my *General Management* anchor is not strong)

- I often want to be more of a generalist than a subject matter expert (as my *Technical Functional* anchor is not strong)

- I might be less interested in a project with a primary deliverable that "does not improve the lives of others" (My *Service* anchor is high). Therefore, I may prefer to work in "*Service* anchor" industries such as healthcare or biotechnology

Knowledge of Your Preferred Role on a Team

A third approach you can use to discover more about yourself is to look at the role you prefer to play on a team. This process can be quite telling, regardless of any formal role title that you have on the team.

Parker (2003) has devised an interesting typology for defining the four primary roles often present on a team. To varying degrees of success, you will likely be able to function in each of these four roles. However, one or two of the roles will likely suit you best. Parker's roles, with my modified descriptions, are as follows:

- **The Collaborator**: The role of ensuring the team keeps its eye on the team's ultimate purpose/goal

- **The Contributor**: The role of keeping the team on task, and focused on the immediate, pressing piece of business

- **The Challenger**: The role of playing devil's advocate, pushing the team towards risk-taking and the pursuit of new paradigms

- **The Communicator**: The role directed towards ensuring the team's interpersonal processes are in place

As with the other approaches to self-knowledge that we have previously examined in this chapter, we can use the Parker system to better understand ourselves. And as before, I will share my most desired Parker team roles (based on my having completed the Parker self-assessment instrument).

My most desired team roles, based on my assessment, are the *Collaborator* and the *Communicator*. With this knowledge in mind, I can deepen my self-knowledge by considering these implications for me:

- *My attraction to the Communicator role:* As team leader, I may be good at focusing on the interpersonal and group-process aspects of the project

- Additionally, I tend to put emphasis on helping the team stay focused on its overall mission (*given my attraction to the Collaborator role*)

- However, I may fall short in my ability to prod the team towards taking appropriate risks (due to my low interest in the *Challenger role*)

- Finally, it is possible I may not be particularly strong at keeping the team focused on the immediate tangible task (*due to my low interest in the Contributor role*)

Thus, the Parker system offers me additional information about myself, in this case what roles I am attracted to when working on a team.

Now, before we go any further in this chapter, having looked at various approaches to knowing ourselves as leaders, I want to offer a few beliefs that I hold dearly when working with these different models of knowing ourselves, and the accompanying implications of "strengths" and "weaknesses." These beliefs are presented below:

- We do not have to be excellent in all aspects of leading

- We just need to know what we are good at, and then find others on the team to compensate for our shortcomings

Having offered this reminder about you not needing to be excellent in all aspects of leadership, let's now return to our focus on presenting additional methods for knowing ourselves. This next model involves knowing ourselves through an understanding and awareness of what have been called the "Big Five" personality factors.

Knowing Yourself Through the "Big Five" Personality Factors

In recent years, personality research, from a number of perspectives, is converging on the belief that says the essence of one's personality can be described in terms of one's functioning along five different dimensions of personality.

A benefit of this five-factor approach is that it is tangible, with five terms that are generally intuitively self-evident. Additionally, the terms hold up well when examined in research settings. The five factors have also been applied to describing optimal team personality combinations (O'Neil and Allen, 2010).

The five factors are: Conscientiousness, Agreeableness, Neuroticism, Extraversion, and Openness. Table 2.1 below provides working definitions for each of the five factors.

Table 2.1

Common Descriptions of the "Big Five" Personality Factors

Personality Factor	Description	Additional Descriptions
Conscientiousness	The extent to which you are careful, scrupulous, and persevering	Competent, disciplined, and deliberate
Agreeableness	Your ability to get along well with others	Straightforward, altruistic, and modest
Extraversion	The tendency for you to experience positive emotions and have a positive outlook about yourself and the world	Gregarious
Neuroticism	The tendency (and degree) for you to experience negative emotional states, and to view yourself and the world around you negatively	Depressive feelings, anxiety, and impulsive tendencies (cognitive or behavioral)
Openness	Willingness to take in new information and perceptions, even when the content of such may not be positive for you	Ability to take in valid criticism from a customer without becoming defensive

Of the five factors, Neuroticism traditionally requires the most definitional explanation for most readers. Neuroticism can be characterized by the presence of negative emotional states, whether chronic or transitory. Such emotional states can include low grade depression, anxiety, and negative self-reflection.

Now, reflect on how you would "score" yourself, through self-assessment, on each of your five factors ("high," "low," etc.).

After you rate yourself, through examination of the five factors as defined in Table 2.1, consider the following conclusions from research on the five factors:

1. The presence of Conscientiousness within individual team members can be a strong predictor of the team's success, or lack thereof. As a result, you as leader want to make sure that:

   • You work hard on role-modeling a conscientious and solid image of yourself

- You work to create an atmosphere, within your team, where accountability, trust, and deliberate follow-through are present

The importance of Conscientiousness, in my view, can be supported through the following explanations: One must possess and promote a common-sense set of work and personal ethics, so that you are perceived as someone that people can count on, operating in a respectful and diligent manner towards all stakeholders.

2.   When you (like all of us) are in a period of "Neuroticism" (i.e., depression and/or anxiety), you may display distinct behaviors that impact your ability (mostly negative) to lead. Consider, for example, the findings of Blanchette and Richards (2010). Among other conclusions, their data suggests that anxiety can lead to the following temporary cognitive impairments:

- Viewing ambiguous situations with greater estimates of risk

- Perceiving facial expressions in a exaggerated negative light

Thus, Blanchette and Richards state that the presence of anxiety appears to create an interpretive bias (i.e., the over-assessing of a situation as threatening). Obviously, such a negative interpretive bias could hinder the team's willingness to risk, as well as the relationship with other teams or customers.

It has been my personal experience that it is very important for one to be cognizant of the negative states like anxiety can have on your performance within the group. When you are anxious, not only does your cognitive functioning suffer, but your interpersonal relationships do as well.

So, how can tell when you are anxious? Below are some classic indicators:

- Edginess or restlessness

- Emotional or physical fatigue

- Difficulty with concentration or short-term memory

- Tense muscles, and/or other somatic issues such as sleeping problems

- Irritability

Clearly, you, I, and every other leader will experience anxiety from time to time. However, it is important that you do your best to prevent anxiety from becoming a chronic occurrence. Remember that when anxiety symptoms do appear, your higher order cognitive functions will be impacted.

Part of "knowing yourself" involves being able to identify the clues that tell you when you are experiencing anxiety. Obviously, many tools exist for handling anxiety, including, in particular, "resilience," which will be discussed in detail throughout Chapter 6.

Knowing Yourself: A Psychological Framework

As a psychologist, I provide psychotherapy and assessment services to my clients. Like all such providers, I frequently assess where an individual may fall short with regard to their general functioning.

Often, this involves examining a person's ability to function in a variety of different areas. Included in these areas are the presence of any current problematic emotions, character traits that might be influencing his/her behavior, the presence of current medical conditions, and any environmental stressors that may be impacting the person's functioning.

With the goal of this chapter of you learning more about yourself, you can assess your own current level of functioning in each of the functional areas just mentioned.

Below, I present these measures of current functioning that I address (as a psychologist) when examining an individual's current level of functioning. As you read the content below, please consider how you would assess your current level of functioning in each of these areas.

If you see areas of functioning in which you are not doing well (now or in the future), then you can use this heightened self-awareness to guide or modify your leadership behavior when appropriate.

Here is a list of possible functional areas in your life that at times can become problem areas:

Are You Experiencing Current Problematic Emotions?

Possible example: Experiencing intense emotional states such as anxiety or depression or having trouble concentrating.

If this is a problem area for you, here's what you can do to minimize the impact on your leadership skills:

- Acknowledge the presence of these intrusive emotions

- Look for causes for these intrusive emotions

- Identify actions you can take to reduce the level of negative impact (i.e., "reduce my stress")

Character Traits That Might Be Hindering Current Leadership Behavior?

Possible example: You may have character traits or attributes (i.e., anger, blaming tendencies, etc.) that can negatively impact your ability to lead.

If this is a problem area for you, here's what you can do to minimize the impact on your leadership skills:

- Identify the trait (i.e., tendency to blame others when things go wrong)

- Keep this awareness in the forefront of your thoughts

- Get sufficient rest and sleep, so as not to diminish your resistance

Are You Experiencing Any Current Medical Conditions?

Possible example: Are you suffering from a chronic (i.e. diabetes) or current medical condition (pneumonia) that can impact your interpersonal behavior, if not appropriately treated?

If this is a problem area for you, here's what you can do to minimize the impact on your leadership skills:

- Be honest with yourself about the existence of the condition

- Follow all prescribed approaches for treating the condition

Any Social or Environmental Stressors in Your Life?

- Financial problems?

- Relationship problems?

- Housing problems?

Be aware of how these current issues can hinder your performance.

Consider How Your Past Impacts Your Present

Obviously, we all are impacted by our past. Good times, bad times, financial hardships, upsetting experiences—the list can go on and on. With this in mind, here are three key points of reference when considering the impact your past has on your present:

1. If you have experienced trauma (or any sort of abuse) in your past, be sure to apply the resources available to you, as unaddressed trauma can be both personally painful and professionally limiting (i.e., apprehensions about conflict situations, interpersonal withdrawal when anxious, etc.).

Individuals who have experienced trauma often have a number of challenges that others might not face. Some symptoms often experienced by victims of trauma include issues with trusting others, a hindered self-concept ("Maybe there was something I did to warrant the abusive treatment"), and hesitation in forming interpersonal relationships, both personal and professional.

Victims of trauma may face unique challenges in the new, emerging project milieus (including working within Agile environments or on cross-national teams). These settings require a great deal of interpersonal flexibility, dexterity, and comfort. Fortunately, there are an increasing number of powerful resources for victims of trauma that significantly aid in the processing of the trauma, allowing individuals to return to optimal levels of performance (Shapiro, 2012).

> I myself have experienced a traumatic event that impacted my functioning dramatically—in the areas of my higher level cognition, short term memory, and the ability to make decisions. I was involved in a catastrophic residential fire, and until I pursued assistance for my posttraumatic symptoms (cognition, memory, decision making), it was a

challenge for me to perform at my best. A variety of resources (Shapiro, 2012) helped me process the event and move forward.

2. Remember that coping approaches that have worked well for you in the past (denial, or interpersonal withdrawal) may, for whatever reason, cease to be as helpful as they were in the past. Therefore, it is important that you stay on top of how you are presently coping with difficult situations, and watch for the natural tendency to continue using coping strategies that may have lost their effectiveness.

3. Just because you've left a nasty work situation behind by taking a different job (leaving a verbally aggressive manager or other stakeholder, or an organization known for mediocre systems for resolving normal conflict, etc.), don't assume that you will not bring some of your difficult feelings with you into the new work setting or team. Take stock of your "bruises," actively doing what you can to work through them, instead of simply bringing them along with you to the new job.

Articulating *Your View* of Human Nature

If you are like most of us, you may not take a great deal of time during your busy week to examine and articulate to yourself your view of human nature. If this is the case, there is nothing wrong. Life and projectized work are demanding enough, and many of us do not have either the time or the inclination to look at these subtle philosophical belief systems.

So, why then, as leader, is it important for you to articulate (at least to yourself) your views on human nature?

The truth is, your beliefs on human nature will color the actions you take as leader, even without your conscious awareness. If you don't have a handle on what you believe about the nature of people, you may operate with a significant blind spot. In many ways, this can hinder your ability to interact interpersonally, motivate others, understand the intentions of other group members, and adequately resolve conflicts.

Obviously, at least in my opinion, there is no correct, singular view on what constitutes the core of human nature. Regardless, whatever you believe about the essence of human nature will influence your approach to leadership.

To further grasp the impact that one's belief systems have on how one approaches others, consider this random assortment of possible beliefs:

- People are motivated by carrots, and not by sticks

- We are all born into original sin

- People are just out for their own self-interest

- There is one correct ethical way to live, and I just happen to know what it is

Having looked at these arbitrarily-presented views of the human condition, please then consider the impact that each of these beliefs might have on leadership. (I will not offer my thoughts on the leadership implications for these beliefs on human nature, due to the fact that my opinion does not matter. What's most important here is what *you* believe).

Hopefully, these random beliefs (certainly not covering the extent of all possible belief systems), will serve one important purpose: to stimulate your exploration of what *you* really believe about human nature.

The more awareness of your belief systems you possess, the more informed you are about what makes you tick. As this chapter has attempted to convey, the use of different models and approaches help you know more about who you are. And as a result, you will perform better as the leader.

Knowing Yourself: Closing Thoughts

In this chapter, I have presented a sampling of approaches that I and others have found meaningful and useful in better knowing one's self.

The goal of this chapter has been to demonstrate the importance of knowing yourself—strengths, weaknesses, vulnerabilities, personal attributes—in order to garner a strong basis for developing your leadership potential.

However, if you choose not to actively focus on knowing yourself, your ability to lead will be significantly hampered, and your growth as a leader will be stunted.

My Self-Awareness Reflections:
Examples of How You Can Use these Approaches

In an effort to illustrate the approaches I have presented in this chapter, I offer Table 2.2 as a detailed summary of what I believe are my own personal self-assessment "findings" and reflections.

In this overview, I use the "data" from my various personal attributes, as discussed earlier, to illustrate how you can grasp the important aspects of who you are as a person by creating your own similar summary.

Additionally, by creating your own summary, you then have a cheat sheet you can refer to from time to time, taking stock about whether or not you are staying open to the processes meant to help you develop a well-defined, current self-knowledge.

Table 2.2

Example of Author Using His Personality "Measures" to Gain Self -Knowledge

Personality "Measure"	Author's Individual "Results"	Positive Implications for Leading	Negative Implications for Leading
Myers-Briggs Type Indicator (MBTI)	Introversion	Good listener. Will not dominate team meetings	May keep too many thoughts and ideas to himself
	iNtuition	Good at seeing the big picture	Could be perceived as "too theoretical"
	Feeling	Empathy	"Too soft"
	Judging	Planful and goal directed	"Too structured"
"Big Five" Personality Attributes	Lack of extroversion	Will allow others to have high profile	May be perceived as "too quiet"
	Tendency towards melancholy	Looks for potential problems	May withdraw from others when stressed
Psychological Functioning Measures			
Problematic current *emotions*?	*Yes*: Feeling anxious and problem focused	Working long hours; very goal directed	Anxiety may hinder performance
Character traits causing issues?	*Yes*: Trust issues are surfacing	Is realistic, and can be demanding of suppliers	Problems with delegating
Current *medical* issues?	*Yes*: Headaches when stressed	?	Difficulty in really listening to others
Current social or *environmental stress*?	*None currently*	Stability in personal life	?

Table 2.3 is a continuation of the summary of my "data," this time presenting materials related to my views of human nature, some thoughts on how my history has impacted my personality, and my work-related values.

Table 2.3

Example of Author Using His Awareness of His Values and Personal History to Gain Further Self Knowledge

Source of His Awareness	Author's Specific Value or History	Positive Implications for Him as Leader	Negative Implications for Him as Leader
His Four Highest *Career Anchors*	1. Service	Desire to be a resource for team	May not pay enough attention to task completion
	2. Entrepreneurial Creativity	Creates atmosphere of possibility and energy	Perceived as "disengaged" as project matures?
	3. Lifestyle	Balance helps him maintain perspective	Customers might "want more" out of him
	4. Autonomy	Operates well in a virtual environment	Not enough of a "team player?"
Key Events in *His History*			
Trauma	Key losses (deaths, plus loss of house to fire)	May have comfort during project recovery efforts	Could focus too much on "what could go wrong" on the project
Coping approaches that may no longer be as adaptive as before	Withdrawing when upset, or when in difficult periods	Gives him time to manage his feelings, and not "strike out" towards others	During problem periods, may appear "aloof" to team members
Previous work experiences impacting his outlook	Once worked for a manager who was verbally abusive	Reminds him of the need to treat all stakeholders with respect	May shy away from giving bad news to "bosses"
His view of human nature	Each person needs to define his/her own individual purpose in life	Could help him assist team members in identifying their goals for the project	Might be perceived as "focusing too much on what team members want," and not enough on the mission.

Knowing Yourself: A Journey With No End

It is very important that you know yourself, as you will not be an effective leader unless you have an ongoing, working knowledge of who you are as a person.

There is no one way to know yourself.

In this chapter I have offered approaches I find very helpful. There are also countless other approaches you can choose to adopt.

Remember, the process of knowing yourself is not the search for a fixed essence of who you are. Said differently, there are no smoking guns or fixed personality attributes to be found. Rather, acknowledge that you are constantly changing and periodically take stock.

I'm always amazed at how much new information one can gather by posing the question, "Who am I today, and what do I believe in?"

Chapter 3
How to Make Personal Changes

Steven Flannes

Obviously, this book is about expanding your leadership skills. But to develop new skills, you often have to first make personal changes. This is often difficult. So, in this chapter, I describe how you can make the personal changes needed for you improving your competencies in the required leadership skills.

Here is a key belief I have:

- If you are going to be a successful leader in the next generation, you need to be comfortable with constantly making significant personal changes. This ability to make personal changes facilitates your ability to develop leadership skills.

The changes I am referring to here do not involve your acquiring additional technical competencies (although such skill acquisition is certainly important).

Rather, what I am talking about here is the interpersonally demanding process of continually updating, changing, and modifying your interpersonal skill sets.

This is not an easy process, and it takes courage, self-reflection, and the willingness to risk. Making personal changes is not a one-time effort. Instead, it is a commitment to a way of being, one of openness, flexibility, and the willingness to embrace new ways of defining who you are.

The need for these changes is grounded in enterprise challenges. As I discussed in Chapter 1, the world is rapidly changing and cross-national work is increasing, as is the complexity of your tasks. Thus, you must change, and change often. Embrace the process of developing your internal self, as the rewards from that way of being transcend just the immediate workplace. You will then also be better equipped to enjoy your identity as a "citizen of the world."

A Perspective on Personal Change

As adults, we are a bit of a finished product in terms of our personality, and our general view of who we are, and how we fit into the world.

Thus, it is often difficult to see how we can make substantive change in who we are. Consider how many times you have heard, or have uttered the phrase yourself, that "people don't really change who they are."

That may be true, but we can still make important changes "around the edges" of who we are, and we will be able to reap big rewards.

Consequently, the idea here is not to attempt to change the basic essence of who we are, but to make additions to a fluid definition of ourselves.

The process is like keeping the same house you've had for a while, but subtracting old furniture, adding a new roof, and painting the exterior. These efforts will change the functionality (i.e. fewer leaks in the roof) as well as the attitudinal environment (what it feels like to be there) of your house.

And that is what you want for yourself: to be able to make personal modifications that change your leadership functionality as well as your attitudinal grounding.

As you have seen so far, the basic theme of this book, and this chapter in particular, is as follows:

1. Leaders with increasing levels of expertise in the interpersonal skills of leadership gain such expertise by making crucial "internal" changes in outlook, self-concept, and the willingness to interpersonally risk.

2. The acquisition of leadership skills cannot come primarily from "external" mediums such as books, classes, or seminars (This idea will be expanded upon below).

3. This "internal work" done by the leader is a prerequisite for the leader's ability to manage teams in our world of project and cross-cultural complexity.

Interestingly, you will find that none of the approaches presented in this chapter are unique to any one individual school of thought. In fact, the power of these approaches is due in large part to their efficacy across generations, cultures, and belief systems. When these approaches are actively embraced, they form a powerful platform from which you can venture into the ongoing process of making the changes required for increasing your soft skills of leadership.

Change Starts with an Internal Focus

As stated above, I believe that the process of expanding your soft skills is an "internal based" function, involved with modifying your internal psychological makeup. This internal focus, exemplified by examining your thoughts, feelings, beliefs, fears, and goals, serves as the foundation for personal change.

Solely trying to make personal change via an "external" focus (i.e., adding skills by reading books, attending classes and seminars) results in minimal to moderate success.

Even though I am a provider of such "external" methods for developing soft skills (writing, seminars, etc.), I must admit to the following: Trying to make changes exclusively through these external methods will result in superficial leadership skill enhancement.

So, what are the specific core beliefs that guide my philosophy regarding making personal change?

I have three core beliefs, and they are presented below:

1. You must be willing to be aggressively self-reflective, taking an honest inventory of who you really are. That's a focus not on your role or title, but on who you really are as a person.

2. You are responsible for your behavior and feelings, as well as your motivation to change yourself.

3. And finally, you must display an ongoing courage to try new behaviors, coupled with an acceptance that personal pain is part of this developmental process.

These fundamental processes for making personal changes (and their benefits) are outlined in Table 3.1.

Table 3.1

Basic Steps for Making the Personal Changes Needed for Leadership Enhancement

Core Steps for Making Personal Changes	Frequent Resistance to Taking the Action Implied in this Step	Benefit to Taking the Action Implied in this Step
Step 1: Take an honest, current inventory of your interpersonal strengths and weaknesses	*"I know myself pretty well. I've been in this business for a number of years. And I've been successful, too."*	World of work is changing at an incredibly fast pace, with greater technological and cross-cultural complexity than ever before
Step 2: Take personal responsibility for your motivation to change and develop	*"If the company wants me to change, then they'll send me for more training. Besides, I'm too busy; I'm not looking for extra things to do."*	No one really cares whether or not you make changes. If you don't take responsibility for the change process, and own the motivation to make it happen, you will be left behind.
Step 3: Find the courage to challenge yourself, to risk, and to engage in new behaviors	*"I push myself enough as it is, just trying to get the work done. Why elevate my profile by taking a chance?"*	Personal change does not happen via tidy, predictable, incremental units of effort. Leaps are often required.

Processes Leading to Personal Change

My professional life in psychology, operations leadership, and project management has provided me with rich experiences from which I have developed my beliefs about how you can make significant personal change. I will now share my list of self-directed processes and experiences that I believe help people make changes. This list includes eleven approaches:

1. Define *what* you want to change

2. Ask yourself *why* you want to make this change now

3. Identify the negative price you will pay for not changing

4. Accept that making personal change is a lonely process

5. There is no correct or right way to develop a skill

6. Be aware of self-created impediments to change

7. Use paradox and humor to help get you started

8.   Leverage your "individual differences"

9.   Involve your heart, your body, and your head in the change process

10. Focus on your *behavior*, and not the outcome

11. View your change process as a series of iterations

Each of these eleven approaches is described in some detail below.

What Do You Want to Change?

Making significant personal change, with the goal of increasing your soft skills, is a difficult, frustrating, and painful process. Given that, why not start with the easy part first?

The easy part is defining what it is about you that you want to change. This sounds obvious, but you can get stuck right from the start if you do not really think through the details of your goal.

For example, I might say that I desire to "improve my ability to address conflict." Clearly, this is a good goal, and is something that we all need in project management.

However, the limitation of this framing of this goal is in the lack of specificity and detail present in its definition. For example, what does it really mean when I say "I want to improve my ability to address conflict?"

My goal regarding "conflict management," and the identification of its concomitant behaviors, must be articulated in a more exacting and detailed manner, so that I have very concrete, behaviorally-based steps that I can use to guide my efforts.

Not defining these behaviors with specificity and detail is similar to having the project goal of producing a deliverable that "improves manufacturing quality." A good goal, clearly, but who really knows what that means?

So, specificity in articulating what I want to change (using the goal mentioned above about me improving my skills in conflict management) can result in something like the following:

> I desire to gain more abilities to manage, in real time, the physical agitation and emotional fear I experience when I am in a discussion involving conflict. Additionally, I need to develop concrete assertive behaviors that will aid my "speaking up," so that I can use some negotiation skills that to date have existed for me mostly on intellectual levels.

Certainly, that's a mouthful, but notice as you read that specific goal if you don't come away with a sense of greater clarity about what it is that I really want to change and develop.

But, please remember that this clarity often does not come the first time you ask yourself for this level of detail. The clarity often emerges as the result of an iterative process in which you notice and reflect upon what is working or not working, followed then by your making efforts to tangibly define your goal.

Why Make Your Change *Now?*

If you are going to ask yourself to reflect, struggle, and risk new behaviors, it is important that you have a clearly articulated personal reason for why you are making the change now.

Attempting to make the change just because someone else wants you to do it is not effective, as we all know from times when others have told us to lose weight, stop smoking, or start exercising. Change really works only when you personally "own" the change effort, identifying deep, personal reasons that you can embrace and that can sustain you as you work through difficult times.

One subjective exercise that I have found helpful for myself and others in defining why to make a change now is a process that has been expanded and nurtured by the late psychologist James Bugental, Ph.D. (Bugental, 1990). This approach is called "your life line." The process involves your drawing a line as follows:

[--]

Here is how the process works:

The left end of the line represents your birth. The right end of the line represents your death.

Now comes the tricky part: place a mark on your life line that you believe represents where you are today in your journey from birth to death. (If you are feeling a bit uneasy about where to place your mark, do as I sometimes do when I am using this exercise: cheat, and make the mark in pencil).

Now, having placed your mark, look at the left side of your mark. This area on your life line represents what you have "lived" to date. Take a few moments to consider your special achievement and accomplishments. Maybe even write them down.

Then, having done that, look at the portion of the line to the right of your mark. This portion of your line represents the amount of time you hope you still have left in your life.

Obviously, you don't know how much time you really have left, nor do you know what is in store for you in the future. And clearly, you have no guarantees about your future opportunities or outcomes. Likely, if you are similar to most other people, looking at this portion of the line creates anxiety and discomfort for you.

But here's the good news.

The unease and the discomfort that arises from this form of uncertainty can serve as motivations. Specifically, as you once again realize that your life will really end, and that you don't know when that will be, you may feel an urgency to make those things happen (changes, experiences, etc.) that you "always planned on getting to someday."

Realizing that you do not know how many "somedays" you have left can help you really identify changes you want to make (and experiences that you want to have in your life), plus the realization that unless you personally take ownership of making such changes, no one else will.

You can also periodically lead yourself through the exercise by just placing yourself in a quiet location, and giving yourself 10 to 15 minutes to move through the exercise.

In concluding this discussion of your life line, it is good to acknowledge the obvious: the ideas underlining it are not new to any of us. However, there definitely is a power to this exercise when done in an unhurried and reflective manner. Often, an exercise like this can remind you of the finitude of your existence, and can create an initial discomfort that can be massaged into a motivation for making changes *now*.

Once you are gone, your legacy fades quickly, so why not try some new things in your life now? If not now, then when?

What Are Your Negative Consequences of *Not* Changing?

Whether we want to admit it or not, most substantive personal change comes from our experiencing pain. Pain is a motivator, and it gets us moving in a way that "positive motivation" does not. Pain helps jolt you out of the trend towards homeostasis and the status quo.

Unfortunately, you may naturally want to deny the presence of your pain. Or, at best, you may want to minimize its presence, rationalizing that its impact on you is just "the cost of doing business," just part of "working for a fast-paced company," or "something that's part of this tough economy." While these truisms may have some legitimacy, they can also be a cognitive self-talk that you may be using to mask the "pain" that you are suffering by not making a change.

And what is this "pain" within the context of project management? Examples are widespread, and can include:

- Chronically high personal stress levels, due to chronic central nervous system activation (Flannes, 2010) as a result of having inadequate skills in saying "no"

- Fear when facing a conflict, feeling "skill-less" to manage a conflictual interaction

- Somatic consequences, such as hindered sleep from "worrying all the time" about tasks that could be delegated (Flannes, 2011)

- Emotional consequences, such as depression or anxiety, from being passive when interacting with interpersonally abusive stakeholders

- A stalled career, due to poor interpersonal skills that contribute to mediocre team cohesion and therefore mediocre project results

Thus, the "pain" you may have can take many forms. Another way of thinking about your pain is to describe it as the negative consequence of you not making important changes.

The question that naturally surfaces as you consider these ideas is: How can you authentically experience and identify the pain that you may be carrying? Here are some processes that may help you identify your pain:

- Give yourself some quiet moments here and there to reflect upon your emotions and your physical functions and abilities. Depressed? Anxious? Feeling hopeless? Feeling cynical? Overly tired? Weight gain or weight loss?

Poor sleeping? Body ache? Lack of motivation? Resignation or give-up feelings?

- The information you get from these reflections tells you the price you are paying from something that is dysfunctional in your life. Seeing the toll you pay for not having made previous changes can be a catalyst for taking action.

- Ask trusted others for feedback regarding their perceptions of your emotional, attitudinal, and physical functioning, in terms of risk areas that these other people may see in those aspects of your functioning.

- You may or may not be someone who finds it helpful to think out loud with a neutral party about these types of prices that you are paying. If you are such a person, consider finding a counselor/advisor to help you continue to identify the negative consequences of the pain, and to partner with you in identifying a path towards creating skills that will alleviate the pain. Such advisors can be professional coaches and personal counselors or psychotherapists.

Accept the Idea that Personal Change is a Lonely Business

One of the fallacies that an individual may hold onto when considering making a substantive personal change is the desire to do so only if one can find someone else who can "really understand me and what I'm going through."

Waiting "to be understood" when considering making personal change is a losing mindset because no one will ever know the challenges you will face except you. Others are just not able to fully grasp the difficulty in making your desired changes, nor the struggles that you will face. So, give up looking for someone who can do that.

However, certainly look for people with whom you can *partner* in making your changes, but let go of hoping to be truly understood. You, as all others, will be fundamentally alone in your effort.

To handle this dilemma of "being alone," you may gain solace in knowing that this "not being understood" is just part of life and change making, and you can learn to trust your own instincts when stepping into the unknown terrain of personal change. By definition, making personal change is a journey fraught with uncertainty, fear, isolation, and the requirement to step solitarily into the unknown.

There Is No "Right Way" to Make Personal Changes

There is no right path to follow. So, you have to make a choice and take action.

You must pick a direction, engage in it, and see how it works. Waiting for someone else (your boss, the PMBOK guidelines, or a peer) to define the direction you "need to take" will result in a status quo. In reality, most people are too wrapped up in their own worries and concerns to be capable of defining a new path that you should take, even if they were interested in doing so.

Do *something,* try a new approach, and risk presenting a new behavior to stakeholders.

Self-Created Cognitive Impediments to Change

As you try new behaviors in service of making changes, watch for two self-created and powerful impediments to getting started. These impediments are "what if" thinking and the adoption of "maladaptive Type A Behavior."

"What if thinking" is that process where you focus too strongly on what *could* go wrong if you tried something new. For example, in working on developing new conflict resolution skills, here are what if cognitions that could stop you in your tracks:

- "*What if* I am more assertive during the next team meeting, and the team becomes irritated with me?"

- "I could try 'saying no' more often to the project sponsor, *but what if* she gets angry with me? Will that derail my career?"

What is the antidote to the paralyzing aspect of *what if thinking*?

Start by briefly considering the possible negative consequences of a new behavior, and then immediately shift to a cognitive mindset that says, in essence, "Should that negative thing happen, I'll trust myself that I'll be able at that point to come up with an appropriate response."

This type of mindset does not involve denial or an overly optimistic outlook. Instead, what it does do is reinforce the mindset that you can have a basic confidence in yourself to successfully address situations that may arise, should unexpected issues surface. Examples of phrases that are variants of this mindset are:

- "If my car does break down on the trip, I'm sure there will be someone I can find to help me figure out what happened"

- "I really hope that it does not rain during our beach trip to the Caribbean, but if it does, I'm sure we'll be able to find some other things to do that we'll enjoy"

The other mindset that limits you when you are trying to make changes is the concept of Type A Behavior. This intense way of being is a behavior that all of us engage in from time to time, but some more than others.

For our purposes, I define Type A Behavior as consisting of:

1. A drive for perfection in implementing existing or new behaviors

2. A subjectively experienced sense of chronic time urgency, regardless of the task, its importance, or the context in which you are operating

3. A chronic, free-floating crabbiness, irritation, or interpersonal "edge" (that may be the result of numbers 1 and 2 above)

Cumulatively, a goal for perfection in your new skill may hold you back from taking any action, and keep you stuck where you are. Perfectionism, then, holds you back because your effort at trying something new becomes framed as an all-or-none cognition: either I do the new skill correctly, or I don't. Such all-or-none thinking creates a situation where you will have much less motivation for trying something new. You may easily hold yourself back.

Consider this example: if you desire to learn to ski, it is probably more likely that you will really show up on the snow if you have performance expectations that are framed in non-absolutist terms. Conversely, if you believe you should do it "right" the first time on snow, you are likely to not leave the lodge.

On a positive note, there is a nice alternative for those of us who fall prey to our own Type A Behavior.

When considering trying something new, an alternative to the implied perfectionism of Type A Behavior is what some people are describing as "adaptive" Type A Behavior. This mindset requires a cognitive shift, where you still aim high in terms of your performance, but these are goals, not absolutes.

Thus, if you try a new behavior, you are aiming for a "quality" effort, and not "perfection." Additionally, adaptive Type A Behavior involves the ability to not criticize yourself should you not achieve your idealized level of performance when you implement your new behavior.

Therefore, when trying to identify your own self-imposed impediments to making changes, please remember these suggestions:

- Watch that your concern about the future consequences of your behavior does not get out of hand and create paralysis for you in the here-and-now.

- Have *goals* for your new personal skill, but be gentle with yourself when you don't hit "perfection" in its implementation.

Use Paradox or Humor to Get You Started

So far in this chapter, I have identified certain mindsets or approaches that can be self-limiting. These mindsets are traction killers when you are considering making a personal change.

An approach that moderates the impact of such staying-stuck mindsets is the application of paradox, irony, or humor. The classic example of someone who applies the meld of paradox/irony/humor towards getting started in making a change, or adopting a new behavior, is the infamous person who is reputed to have said:

- "When I'm on my death bed, will I really care that I tried a new approach to conflict management during the middle of my career, and the result wasn't quite what I hoped for?"

Such a statement encourages you to step away from immediate anxieties or fears, and look at the big picture, or the overall arc of your life, hopefully gaining awareness that what seems like a huge action or risk today, probably, in the totality of your life, is not that ultimately significant.

To be effective in using paradox/irony/humor, you need to find (or create) a cognition that has personal resonance or enjoyment for yourself. In other words, the cognition that you use (to lighten you up and make things seem less intense) must be something that you can readily access in time of need, such as an humorous image that you can visualize, or an idea that brings a small smile to your face when you silently repeat it to yourself in service of taking a chance.

While change is difficult, there is no reason that you can't add some humor to it. By applying a humorous image or by employing paradox, you can reduce your apprehension and anxiety, which will make trying something new much easier.

Leverage Your "Individual Differences"

The concept of individual differences comes from psychology and the study of personality. Basically, the concept states that while a group may appear homogenous in nature when viewed from one perspective (such as a group of software engineers all with six years of service), it can also be viewed as a group of "individuals" who bring "differences" in variables such as temperament, beliefs, and communication style.

Within the project management world, the concept of individual differences has been described and applied as a method to craft best practices when communicating with team members or when crafting motivation approaches (Flannes and Levin, 2005). One popular model for identifying and applying individual differences in a team environment has been the Myers-Briggs Type Indicator (MBTI).

You can apply your knowledge of your four MBTI preferences (i.e., your own "individual differences," or uniqueness) to identifying your own best practices when you are embarking on a process of trying to make substantive personal change.

Listed below are best practices for making personal changes for each of the eight MBTI preferences.

- **Extravert:** Talk and interact with others about how they make changes. Put yourself in group settings and try out new behaviors

- **Introvert:** Give yourself some quiet time to reflect and visualize your desired new behavior, and then practice it in small, intimate settings

- **Sensing:** Identify concrete, tangible behaviors that you can list, and then practice. Stay focused on the long term and do not pay too much attention to short term "failures"

- **Intuition:** Visualize how you eventually want to change and come across to others, but also hold yourself accountable for making some concrete efforts in the short term

- **Thinking:** Look for logical reasons for taking chances in trying out new behaviors. Also, remember that being aware of your feelings is also important in making changes, so don't do too much just in your head

- **Feeling:** Allow yourself to feel the subjective benefit of making your change ("It will be so good to feel less anxious during a conflict!') but don't get lost in your feelings. Use your head to craft a short list of behaviors to try, and implement the list whether or not you "feel like it"

- **Perceiving:** You will be good at "going with the flow," being flexible in trying new behaviors. And, be sure to also set some time lines to mark your actual implementation of the desired new behavior

- **Judging:** You will be good at creating lists of new behaviors to try, but watch for the tendency to *not really try* new things. Also, guard for the belief that "if it is not broken, don't fix it"

Tap Into the Meld of Your Mind, Body, and Spirit

Personal change occurs most readily if you access more than one channel for facilitating the change. The best of all situations is one in which you are working on the change by employing the cognitive, emotional, and physical channels that we all possess.

An example of using all three of these channels in concert with each other might look something like the plan described below:

1. "During my run today, I will focus on my sense of body strength and see if I can imagine using this physical energy to propel me into trying my new behaviors" (physical)

2. "As I run, I will try to silently enumerate a few reasons (cognitive) on how my new, evolving behavior will make my job easier and more efficient"

3. "And finally, as I'm running, I'll also take some time to casually identify which of my feelings (emotional) I want to modify, such as "feeling less anxious during confrontations"

By trying to embrace each of these channels of awareness, you can intensify the energy behind your motivation to change.

Focus on Your *Behavior,* and Not the *Outcome*

Personal change, done on a substantive level, is hard work, drawing down your emotional and physical energies, while also challenging your previously held views of your self-concept and how the world works.

A very important mindset that lightens the load when making changes is the approach of focusing on your *behavior*, and not the *outcome*. By focusing on your behavior, you are applying yourself in the moment, addressing the aspect of change over which you have some control, that being your behavior at any one moment.

Conversely, if you focus too much on a possible outcome ("Will these behaviors be effective in solving my conflict with Andrew?"), you will find that you will be operating in a time and space continuum (the future) over which you have no control. Your focusing on these no-control situations creates anxiety that hinders your taking action.

Instead, focus on the details of the behavior that you want to employ. For example, if you are working on conflict resolution skills, your focusing on the *behavior*, instead of the *outcome*, might look something like this:

1. Make eye contact with Andrew

2. Take a few deep breaths

3. Mention you have a situation that needs to be addressed

4. State your opinion

5. Ask Andrew for his opinion

6. Look for points the two of you share in common

7. Create a method you both will use to address the areas in which you both still disagree

And so forth…

By creating such a list of behavioral actions, you simplify your expectations of yourself; all you then need to do is implement the actions. Let the resolution of the conflict, or the lack of resolution, take care of itself. You cannot control that result. Throw your energy into what you can affect, that being your taking action.

View Your Change Processes as a Series of "Celebrated" Iterations

When you make changes, you feel uncertain, awkward, and fearful about how your efforts will turn out, as well as wondering what others will think about you.

Consequently, you need to experience some positive feedback or reinforcement, and it makes no difference even if *you* are the one to provide it. So, aim to identify the very smallest reasons to celebrate any effort you make into uncertain waters. Celebrate, honor, and acknowledge that you tried something. The celebration does not need to be big or even noticeable to others.

There's no point in your waiting to celebrate until you "do it right," as you will probably never be able to know when you've "done it right." Below is an example of a small "celebration" in service of one leader who was working on being more assertive:

- **Behavior:** Spoke up during a team meeting when he perceived an unidentified conflict among team members

- **Celebration:** Treated himself to an afternoon coffee

- **Benefit of the celebration:** Allowed him to spend ten minutes of uninterrupted time reflecting upon how good it felt to speak up in the meeting

Clearly, this idea of celebrating small steps and progress is an example of enjoying the journey. There is "always more" in the realm of making personal change, so why not enjoy the process by celebrating the many small steps along the way? If you don't throw these celebrations for yourself, no one else will.

Closing Thoughts

As I have said, true personal change initiates internally, through your self-directed processes of:

- Defining your goal
- Taking risks
- Experiential learning
- Counseling-like relationships
- The willingness to trust yourself in trying new approaches

This chapter has addressed a variety or processes and behaviors that assist you in initiating or jump starting a change process that you have identified as important to you. These ten processes and behaviors are summarized in Table 3.2.

Table 3.2
Summary: Processes that Can Assist You in Making Personal Changes

Process or Behavior	Example of Tangible Goal	Tips to Help You Apply this Process or Behavior
Define *what* you want to change	"In conflict situations, I want to be less physically agitated and more comfortable in tolerating ambiguity."	Identify one deep breathing exercise that can help calm your physiology. Define one benefit to "being more comfortable."
Articulate *why* you want to make the change *now*	"My last three projects suffered in the quality area because I did not address conflicts on the team."	Write down two examples of how I would have been more successful if I had better conflict management skills.
Identify the price you will pay for not changing	My career goal of becoming a program manager seems to be stalled because "I don't handle conflict well."	Find out how much more money you'd make if you were a program manager. See how many program manager jobs are out there.
Accept that making change is a lonely process	"I need to remember that I'm working on these changes for *me*, and for the quality of my career."	Remember this idea: I'm the only one who can drive my life forward.
Accept that there is *no "right" way* to make a change	"I'll just try a few conflict management techniques and see how it goes."	Don't let the goal of being "perfect" keep you from achieving the result of being "good."
Be aware of self-imposed *impediments* to making change	"Frequently, I end up not trying anything new because I believe I must do it perfectly."	Make a list of all of the things in life you have *not experienced* because you were concerned with "doing it right."
Use paradox and humor	"If I don't try making these changes soon, I'll be too old and forgetful to enjoy their benefit."	Try doing the life line exercise once a week for one month.
Leverage your "individual differences"	"As an extravert, I'll talk a lot with others about how they manage conflict."	Make a list of five people you know who you believe are good at managing conflict. Schedule one person per week for coffee, and seek ideas and suggestions.
Involve your head, heart, and body	"When I'm on the treadmill at the gym, I'll try to visualize the desired new behavior."	Just show up at the gym, get on the treadmill, and abandon any expectations about how it will go.
Focus on your *behavior*, and not the *outcome*	"My only goal right now is to just try something new. I'll address the results of the behavior later."	Identify your first step in trying a new behavior. Implement it. Repeat. Trust that the outcome will take care of itself.

Making Changes: No One Likes to Do This

Personally, I don't believe that anyone likes to "make changes," as that phrase often connotes the idea of giving something up. What I do believe, however, is that many people enjoy:

- Learning something new

- Feeling better about themselves

- Feeling less stuck, both professionally and personally

These three bullet points above illustrate how you can reframe the change process. This reframing might suggest to you ways you can personally change the tone you associate with your "making changes." Importantly, such a change of tone makes the entire process more appealing.

There's nothing wrong with that!

Chapter 4
Interpersonal Communication:
Skills for the Global Leader

Steven Flannes

This chapter provides you with the specific interpersonal skills needed to lead all stakeholders, as well as suggestions about how you can develop each of these skills. In essence, you will find within this chapter a number of concrete tools that constitute your interpersonal "tool box."

Concrete and Tangible Skills

Personally, I believe it is very important for us to focus on *specific interpersonal skills*. Too often, books, journal articles, and subject matter experts, when addressing the importance of interpersonal components of leadership, often talk "about" the topic, rather than directly defining and articulating the specific skills.

For example, leaders are often encouraged to "be good communicators" or "treat people with respect." Unfortunately, when skills are discussed in this "about" manner (i.e., one that is descriptive in nature as compared to behavior-specific), you are left with nothing tangible to work towards or practice when endeavoring to develop these skills.

Therefore, the goal of this chapter is to present distinct interpersonal skills that you can both conceptualize and practice. Hopefully, the clarity of this approach will make this component of leadership appear more tangible and developmentally accessible.

Required Leader Communication Skills

To be an effective communicator, you need to first have an awareness of certain values and beliefs that serve as the foundation for quality communication.

Core Belief: Consider the "Alliance and the Context"

Describing the "right" thing to do or say is simply not possible for any one given theoretical situation. For example, an individual in my people skills seminars may ask what they should say, for example, when someone treats them aggressively.

Well, the *right* thing to say is always a function of the nature of the *alliance*, defined as the type of the relationship between the two people. Additionally, the right thing to say also considers the *context*, which relates to the setting or conditions within which the communication is taking place. The noted psychologist Jim Bugental, Ph.D. (1990) was very effective in stressing the importance of these two communication variables.

Alliance refers to the nature of the relationship, such as whether those currently in communication are friends, business partners, or customers, etc. Alliances are fluid in nature, and vary in the degree of comfort, intimacy, openness, trust, shared history, and common goals. Being aware of the alliance's nature offers the chance to tailor communication towards the intricacies and specifics of the immediate communication.

Context variables, on the other hand, can include the setting (whether the message is being delivered in front of a group of project stakeholders or over a casual lunch at a neighborhood cafe) as well as other environmental circumstances (such as operating within in a pressurized workplace following large layoffs).

Obviously, the concepts of alliance and context are grounded in common sense. However, we often do not pay enough attention to their impact when we are initiating a communication with another person. Before we start to communicate, if we can pause for just a moment and consider how the variables of alliance and context may flavor the communication, we can then create messages that are more effectively received by the other person.

Developing Tangible Communication Skills

To be an effective leader, you must be skilled in four fundamental interpersonal communication techniques. These techniques have been described previously in detail (Flannes and Levin, 2005). Due to their foundational importance, they are summarized in following sections.

In addition, the leader needs to have an awareness of subtle communication tone and texture variables present during a communication. Such variables can help the leader "hear" the often unspoken messages coming from the other person. These variables are also discussed below.

Finally, the leader must also have developed a working level of emotional intelligence. Emotional intelligence, or EQ, has been described by researchers from many countries as the most important basic leadership competency (Simic, Nesic, and Arsenijevic, 2012, and Tang, Yin, and Nelson, 2010).

Four Basic Interpersonal Communication Techniques

Remember, to be an effective leader, you do not necessarily need to be "really good" with these four skills. In fact, your making even small improvements in these skills can markedly improve your communication effectiveness.

The skills are presented below in order of complexity (from least to most), and as a function of the degree of "emotional dexterity" required of you for successful application. These required communication skills are as follows:

- Using open-ended questions
- Providing active listening feedback to others
- Tracking the goal-directed thread of a conversation
- Re-framing a negative conceptualization into a more neutral or positive conceptualization

Asking Open-Ended Questions for Information Gathering and Relationship Enhancement

An open-ended question is a question that cannot be answered with a simple "yes" or "no." One example of an open-ended question could be:

> "Please describe the state of progress on the allocation of the additional resources."

Open-ended questions provide you with the opportunity to gather a great deal of information from the other person. Additionally, open-ended questions, when asked in a neutral manner with no hidden agenda, often provide the feeling of "being listened to" for the other party.

You should be careful to not overuse any of the four communication skills. Overuse can create problems. Specifically, there are a number of risks inherent in using too many open-ended questions. What are these risks?

First, one may risk coming across as indirect or unfocused. Even worse, there is the possibility of being viewed as having a hidden agenda. Also, excessive use of open-ended questions can stall the pace of problem solving and forward movement. This may result in an increasing level of frustration for the other person.

While open-ended questions are simple in concept, they are often challenging in execution. For example, you might enter a conversation feeling a sense of time urgency, but such urgency can hinder you having the "cognitive openness" necessary in asking open-ended questions.

Below is a 7-point checklist you can follow when you want to employ open-ended questions.

1. Take a few deep breaths and clear your thoughts (Allows a cognitive openness to exist)

2. Make eye contact with the other person (Assists in truly "hearing" the message of the other person)

3. Before beginning to speak, pause for a few seconds (Helps you settle into the posture of being a "good listener")

4. Access your genuine interest or curiosity for what the other person is saying (Makes it easier to stay involved cognitively if you can find an aspect of the topic that genuinely interests you)

5. Consider the "alliance and context" (Assists you in reading cues about how the conversation is going)

6. Internally track the progress of the conversation, asking yourself if you are getting the information you need (Helps you understand the appropriate time to suspend using open-ended questions, and when to shift to a goal-oriented conversational style)

7. Decide what direction the discussion needs to take (Helps remove you from being stuck in an overly passive posture of using too many open-ended questions)

Like all of the soft skills of leadership, the ability to skillfully apply open-ended questions can be practiced and refined.

Remember: The goal in practicing these soft skills of communication is always to reach a competency level of "good," rather than "excellent."

Listed below are a few methods that are effective for practicing open-ended questions.

- In a non-work setting, try conversing with a friend as if you were a television news reporter. Try asking questions that get the other person to describe who, what, where, when, and how.

- Do not use questions that can be answered with a simple "yes" or "no." Rather, employ questions similar to the following three:

1. "Please tell me more about…"

2. "Please describe what is working and not working on the project."

3. "What are your thoughts about next steps?"

Try asking these questions without inserting your opinion on what you are hearing. Simultaneously, you should avoid using declarative statements. Do not agree or disagree, simply continue asking questions that provide you with more data and information.

Listening Actively to the Stakeholder

Active listening involves making statements to the other party, reflecting your perception of what you have heard him or her say. Below is an example of active listening:

> "I'm hearing that you are concerned about our not having enough resources for the project, along with a worry that the schedule is unrealistic. Have I captured the main points of what you are telling me?"

Active listening allows you to accomplish a variety of goals. For example, active listening:

- Gives the other person the message that you are hearing what he or she is saying (without necessarily agreeing with the point)

- Helps clarify the content and direction of the communication, as well as increasing stakeholder involvement through their experience of "being heard" by you

- Is an effective tool to use when the other person has very strong feelings about something and needs to "get it off his or her chest" before continuing with the conversation

As with the previous discussion of open-ended questions, I present below a leader's checklist to follow when you desire to use active listening.

1. Take deep breaths, clear your thoughts, and make eye contact (Creates a cognitive openness for you that allows for better comprehension of what the other person is saying)

2. Suspend your agenda of what "should" be spoken about (Assists in really hearing and encoding the message of the other person)

3. Moderate your desire to make a declarative statement (Holding back on your declarative statements aids the other person in expounding upon their message)

4. Consider the best timing for when to let the other know that you "hear" their message (Good timing for such an "I hear you" comment creates a climate where the other is encouraged to keep speaking)

5. Be authentic and genuine in the manner in which you craft your "I hear you" statements (An authentic re-stating of what you are hearing reduces the risk of your "I hear you" message coming across as robotic and patronizing)

Methods to use to improve your skill in using active listening also involve efforts to practice in non-intense, more casual settings, such as the following:

•   Tell a friend or family member that you want to practice active listening, and request that they speak for a few minutes about a strong personal interest of theirs.

•   At appropriate points, offer active listening comments that reflect the message you believe you are receiving.

•   As the conversation winds down, request feedback about moments where you may have left "active listening," and started offering your own declarative statements.

•   Try the same process with a stranger who you might be sitting next to on the train or during a flight. Again, you have nothing to lose in practicing these skills within this casual and non-work environment.

Gradually, incorporate more of these questions at work, noting what works and what does not work for you. Do not rate yourself on your effectiveness; adopt a neutral attitude in reviewing your results.

Tracking the Linear Thread of the Discussion

"Tracking" is an assertive communication technique that works well in a number of situations. It is particularly helpful when speaking with someone who repeatedly gets off the subject (due to either conscious or unconscious motivations), thus hindering the linear movement of the discussion towards problem closure or action.

One example of a tracking statement is:

> I think we are getting off topic. Let's back up to the point where you were mentioning the cost for the software package. I think that's the point where I started to lose you.

The leader who artfully uses tracking creates an atmosphere of purposive communication. Indeed, tracking is especially effective and appropriate when there is an enterprise crisis, time is of the essence, and all important verbal communication must proceed in a linear manner towards the goal of risk management.

Here is a 5-point checklist for you to follow when you decide to engage in tracking communication.

1. If an urgent situation, determine the goal for the communication (Conceptualizing the goal allows for the creation of the "track" to be pursued in the discussion)

2. Articulate to the other person your sense of the purpose for the communication (Provides parties with a roadmap that both can refer to, thus increasing efficiency during a crisis period)

3. Speak up quickly, as soon as you perceive that the discussion is "getting off track" (This reduces the chance that you will let your frustrations build up, thus moderating the risk that when you do comment on "being off track," you will do so in with an angry tone)

4. Be comfortable making numerous tracking comments during a discussion (People "in need" of tracking often do not get the message the first time you present it)

5. Trust your instincts about needing to be persistent when using tracking (It's your operation/project, and you need to feel that emergent, crisis situations are being actively addressed)

Methods to use in improving your skill in tracking the thread of a business discussion include the following:

- Write down a key "topic" word as a discussion gets started, and see if the flow of this discussion mirrors the subject suggested by that word

- Practice using self-disclosure comments, should you feel you are losing the direction of the discussion. Such self-disclosure comments can include the following:

"I'm lost right now…where is this discussion headed?"

"Let's pause here. Are we still talking about schedules, or have we moved on to another subject?"

Reframing a Negative Point or Attitude

At times, discussions reach a point where communication is faltering, or negative tones have infiltrated the exchange between people. Unless some change takes place, the discussion is likely headed for failure.

In these situations, a valuable communication tool is "reframing." Much as a picture framer will place a new frame around an existing painting to change its tone, you can put a new "frame" around the faltering discussion and create a new sense of optimism or possibility.

Reframing a discussion puts a different spin on the conversation, allowing the participants to see the issues from a different perspective, potentially one filled with more optimism. A reframing comment can look like this:

"Let's face it. If the discussion keeps going in this direction, we are not going to get anything done. What if we look at this situation as an opportunity to build a bridge between the engineering group in the other division and our group?"

Reframing the issue, which can be done by any person in the conversation, involves creative thinking and a willingness to take a chance by offering a new perspective.

When offering a reframing comment, be prepared for some people to remain stuck in the negative and to resist these creative alternatives. Be persistent. You may need to state the same reframing message in a number of different ways before you achieve success.

Here is a 7-point checklist you can use for the application of reframing:

1. Ability to observe that the other person is stuck in either a cognitive loop of negativity ("We've tried all we can do") or a victim's posture ("I'd do more, but no one is getting me what I need")

2. Assertively pausing the conversation (Stops the flow of negativity)

3. Provide active listening, which gives the team member the sense of "being heard," which is different than "being agreed with." (People often need to "feel heard" before they are willing to open themselves up to trying something different)

4. Offer an open-ended question, such as: "What other approaches could be tried?" (Creates an opening for the team member to expand their own cognitive boundaries regarding what is possible)

5. Do not use questions that can be answered with a "yes" or a "no" (Reduces the risk of the conversation stopping in its tracks)

6. Be persistent with open-ended questions (Such persistence may gradually allow the team member to consider new approaches)

7. Ask the team member to "sleep on it" and return the next day with new possibilities (Allows the team member to know that while you will work with him on this issue, you still expect the team member to come up with a solution)

To skillfully reframe a negative tone or attitude in a conversation, use the following two methods:

1. Experiment with phrases such as "What if we tried…"

2. Be a partner in the solution, not the solution provider

A Cultural Caution

What I value most about the four communication skills listed above is the fact that, while they are undeniably *simple,* they are also *sophisticated.* Throughout my career I have presented these skills to project professionals in transnational settings. Many people have told me that these four skills are very helpful.

However, it is important to also keep in mind that each of these four skills may face challenges when applied in certain cultures. For example, open-ended questions and active listening, when presented to an older stakeholder in certain traditional cultures, can be perceived as both disrespectful and intrusive.

So, to avoid making such a cultural error, you should first consider the windows of *alliance* and *context*, discussed earlier in this chapter. Devoting attention to alliance and context will give you a chance to pause, and consider what will work well with this *individual,* within this *setting,* and at *this point in time.*

Having offered this cautionary note, I'd like to end my discussion on these skills by saying that I believe they are the most important and effective interpersonal communication skills you can use. The skills are summarized below in Table 4. 1.

Table 4.1

Summary of Communication Skills Required of Leaders

Specific Skill	Example of a Statement Using this Skill	Benefit of Using this Skill	Leader's Required Emotional Competency
Asking open-ended questions	"Please tell me more about your concerns on the testing."	Demonstrates an interest in the other person, plus provides you with key data or information	A genuine interest to ask sincere questions that are not grounded in an unexpressed agenda
Active listening	"Sounds as if you think we should start the testing sooner, and involve more people?"	Gives the stakeholder the experience of being "heard" while assuring that both parties are talking about the same points	Ability to listen intently to the other person, suspending one's own tendency to formulate a comeback response (even while the other is speaking)
Tracking	"It seems as if we are losing our focus in the discussion. Let's return to your concerns about the testing process."	Assists all parties in staying focused, moving through the discussion in a linear, goal directed manner	Listening for the direction of the discussion, plus the ability to speak up assertively if the conversation gets off point
Reframing	"I realize you feel stuck. What are some additional paths that have not been pursued?"	Acknowledges the frustration of the team member, but keeps open the door for creativity	Ability to not get lost in the other person's frustration or negativity

Additional Communication Techniques

A number of more subtle communication techniques and considerations exist for leaders. These techniques help you elevate your communication skills to greater levels of sophistication and effectiveness, enabling you to better interact in transnational settings. These techniques and their resulting benefits are presented below.

Making Manifest

Imagine you are leading a virtual team meeting and are feeling that the discussion is negative in tone. Too often, the leader having such observations tries to fix the problem by him/herself, without sharing with the team what he/she is observing.

In such a situation, the leader is asking too much of him/herself, taking on too much individual responsibility for the solution. Instead of silently trying to change the tone and direction of the meeting, this project leader can be much more effective by "making manifest" what he/she is observing. Making manifest is similar to the idea of "I will tell it like I see it."

Here is a statement reflective of a leader making manifest her observation:

> "Team, it seems to me like our tone today is pretty negative and we are jumping to many different topics. Do others have a similar impression? OK, so what can we do *right now* to improve our tone and our focus?"

The benefits of "making manifest" comments are greater efficiency of task completion and improved time management.

To work on developing your skills in "making manifest" your observations:

- Remind yourself that your observations are most likely accurate

- Bring up your observations sooner rather than later. The longer you wait to share these types of observations, the harder it becomes

- Remind yourself that such honest, unvarnished comments are not necessarily "negative," but are "descriptive" of the ineffective communication process that you are observing

Using "Yes, and" Comments

You may find yourself in a situation where you want to acknowledge the suggestion of a team member, but would like to say it in a way that sets the tone for looking for additional solutions.

In other words, at that point, you are seeing the benefits of what the other person has just mentioned, but you want the brainstorming to continue. Such a situation is ideal for a "yes, and" statement.

The following is an example (along with my comments about each portion) of the "yes, and" statement:

- "Yes, Phil, that is a good idea about refining the scope."

With this statement, you are providing him with positive feedback, and letting him know you have heard what he said. However, you believe there are better solutions out there, so you then say:

- "And, what are two other approaches that you can think of regarding the scope problem?"

So, the cumulative benefits of "yes, and" comments are that:

- You keep your team member engaged, hopefully positively

- You are also letting the team member know that there may be better solutions to be found

Using "Yes, but" Comments

This form of statement can appear similar to "yes, and" but there is, in fact, quite a significant difference: "Yes, but" comments serve the purpose, intended or not, of shutting down the direction of communication by offering a firm boundary.

An effective (meaning a productive or intended) application of a "yes, but" statement is:

> "Mike, *yes*, you make a good point about the resource limitations, *but* I'm very clear that we will be getting no additional staff for our project."

Such a statement acknowledges that while you heard him, the issue is really a closed one, and you and the team do not need to spend more time discussing it.

Conversely, a negative application of a "yes, but" statement ("negative" in the following example because you didn't really want to shut down the conversation on the topic) is:

> "Jim, I hear what you are saying about resource limitations, but what you said just makes no sense to me."

So, use your "yes, buts" carefully, primarily in situations where you need to set a strong boundary, a limit, or some other form of firm feedback.

Changing Your Physical Posture or Location

Effectiveness in communication can sometimes be mediocre, even when both parties are doing all the right things. You are in such a mediocre discussion when you notice that creativity is flat, the discussion may be circular in nature, or that decisions are not being made.

When involved in this type of communication, you can appropriately shake things up by *altering your physical posture* (if you've been sitting, stand up and wander around the room) or by *changing your physical location* (if you are speaking with a co-located individual in your office, and things are flat, suggest that you move to the conference room, or go sit outside and continue talking).

Changing your physical posture or location can improve communication due to the fact that the context is now different.

In situations where these changes have been made, the environmental cues for both parties are now altered. Frequently, changes in such contextual cues can assist one in accessing a greater cognitive openness, often leading to the identification of previously unseen paths for problem resolution. These "shifts in context cues" illustrate the benefits of the folk wisdom saying that "you'll benefit from a change of scenery."

Use Silence to Make Your Point

Conversations deteriorate into "talk fests" when each party is simultaneously asserting a view, talking over the other person, and/or believing that using more words is better than using fewer.

During situations in which people continually talk over each other, knowledge sharing and/or problem solving may become ineffective. Consider the following example:

Whilst leading a seminar two or three years ago, one member of the group artfully described such situations as examples of "re-loading."

In these circumstances, one person talks, the other person is hardly listening. Instead, the second person is silently "re-loading" and waiting to fire off their next statement as soon as the first person pauses for breath or places a period at the end of a sentence.

In these intense situations, the use of silence can be effective in catching the attention of the other person, altering the dynamics, and bringing the re-loading cycle to an end. Silence often serves the purpose of avoiding putting more wood on the verbal fire.

Generally, if you use silence while maintaining consistent eye contact, the other person will realize that something is different. Simultaneously, silence provides you with a chance to pause, reflect, and then re-focus your attention towards a different, more constructive path.

Use Paradox to Make Your Point

Leadership can feel like a lonely position. This becomes noticed during difficult times when you are trying to get a particular team member (or even the team as a whole) to accept an unpopular position you have taken, or a controversial decision you have made.

Sometimes during these difficult periods, you can help yourself in getting your point across by applying the use of paradox. For example, if the team is arguing that a decision is unfair, and you have done your best to explain your decision, applying a paradoxical injunction might help.

An example of using paradox for your benefit would be to say something like the following:

"What would you do if you were in my shoes and faced this decision?"

This request to paradoxically step out of one mindset ("team member") and into a different mindset ("leader who faces making an unpopular decision") can expand the cognitive openness of the team member. This will hopefully enable the other person to view the situation from a broader perspective, one less individually driven.

However, sometimes using paradox falls flat, and fails to achieve its goal. This happens most frequently when the paradox is offered out of the leader's personal frustration, possibly coming across to the team member in a tone both sarcastic and patronizing.

However, when used selectively, and offered with the right tone, paradox can be a very effective in enhancing communication by breaking up log jams.

Use Time Boundaries as Creators of Urgency and Focus

As a leader, you will undoubtedly face situations in which communication is going well among team members: points are being made clearly, people are listening, and conflict is absent.

However, "nothing is getting done." For whatever reason, discussion is not leading to task completion, decision, or closure. You find yourself wondering what to do to move from communication to action.

The use of time boundaries is an obvious, yet sophisticated interpersonal tool you can apply to create goal-directed communication. An example of a time boundary statement you could use is as follows:

> "Team, we have 7 minutes left in the meeting before we face a hard stop. We must make a decision on the delivery date before we end. What does everyone think the date should be?"

Now, a one-time use of a time boundary statement like the one presented above may not work, so you may need to increase the intensity as well as the sense of urgency, by saying something like:

> "OK, now we only have 5 minutes now. What is our decision?"

And just for the sake of example, here is a third comment, should it be needed:

> "Well, we are now down to just 2 minutes. I'm not sure you've picked up my urgency on this. If I don't get a date from you in the next two minutes, I'll just set one, and you will all have to live with it."

And so it goes.

However, when used too frequently by the leader, this form of communication intervention will be received by others as pushy, simplistic, and controlling. So, use it selectively. My experience has shown me that this intense, pushy, "time-is-urgent" message works best for the leader generally known for having a low-key style.

In addition to the skills noted so far in the chapter, there exists another subtle, yet powerful skill, or interpersonal posture, I'd like to present separately. This skill deserves special attention. This skill is your ability to "be present."

Being "Present" During the Discussion

My experience suggests that the ability to "be present" during conversations is the most important skill one can have for any type of interpersonal interaction.

Being present when communicating suggests a mindset and posture that places emphasis on the thoughts, ideas, feelings, and beliefs *you are experiencing at that specific moment* in the conversation, as well as an awareness of what is going on with the other person.

This ability is characterized by a working awareness of your mood, energy level, cognitions, and emotions. For example: Are you having a good day? Feeling angry? Cognitively distracted?

Having this awareness does not necessarily mean that you have to disclose it to others, nor act upon these feelings when communicating. Rather, the goal is to have a healthy awareness of what is going on with you presently in order to utilize this awareness to communicate more effectively with your team members.

How can you work on actively *being present* during a conversation? Here are two approaches to consider:

- *Reflect on your immediate feelings and cognitions.* Your goal should be to develop an awareness of what you are feeling at that particular moment. Such awareness will help you avoid stepping into conversational potholes as you communicate with others.

- *Reflect on what your body is telling you.* Physical awareness of your current state can provide a tremendous amount of "data" to better understand what is going on with you. Each person may have his or her own set of bodily cues signaling important information about what is taking place emotionally and cognitively.

Your developmental task here is to identify what constitutes *your* cues, and be able to track them during a discussion, so as not to distract you by what is going on internally. This may allow you to concentrate deeply on your discussions with others.

By "being present" in the discussion with another person, you are showing that person that you are:

- Focused on them (and not thinking about your last meeting)

- Being attentive to them (and not scanning your monitor)

- Currently really *available to them* (and are not distracted by your planning how you will get to the airport for your evening flight)

Emotional Intelligence:
An Integrative Interpersonal Skills Model

This chapter has presented communication skills—both tangible and subtle—that serve as the required communication foundation for the next generation leader. Importantly, no amount of a leader's technical skill, strategic vision, or industry knowledge can compensate for a mediocre competency in these interpersonal skills.

At this point in the chapter, I would like to introduce a popular conceptual and research-based model for understanding interpersonal competency. This model is known as emotional intelligence.

Emotional intelligence is a valuable, integrative model, weaving together a number of core skills and abilities that cover the breadth of the interpersonal competencies needed to be a successful leader.

The concept of emotional intelligence (or EQ) gained notoriety through the work of individuals like Daniel Goleman (Goleman, 1995). However, a number of other EQ models are also in existence. For a comprehensive overview of such models, see Bharwaney, Bar-On, and MacKinlay (2011), who interestingly enough, trace the roots of EQ back to the work of great minds like Charles Darwin.

EQ, regardless of the specific model being considered, involves core abilities such as skill in being able to identify the emotions of self and others, and the ability to operate in difficult situations in ways that suggest you can effectively moderate your emotions.

Business cases for the importance of EQ in the workplace suggest that its presence adds significant value. In fact, it is often considered to be more important than IQ and technical skills (Simic, Nesic, and Arsenijevic, 2012). EQ has been described as accounting for differences in leaders's abilities in conflict management and teamwork (Clarke, 2010), as well as abilities in transformational leadership (Malik, Danish, and Munir, 2012).

(As you will see, my treatment in this chapter of EQ is selective, highlighting its ever increasing global acknowledgement. Clearly, it is a skill set that next generation leaders will be hearing more about).

Below, I present recent project management applications in the area of EQ and leadership. Additionally, I will share ideas on how I believe you can expand your EQ capabilities.

EQ in Project Leadership—and Beyond

EQ has been extensively researched (Clarke, 2010 and Davis, 2011). Results from these efforts have suggested that mixed models of EQ are best, and that the project manager's level of EQ significantly impacts the quality of his or her attentiveness.

To get a sense of the global embracing of EQ as a foundation for leadership excellence, take a look at Table 4. 2 This table presents a brief sampling of global efforts to investigate the EQ/leadership relationship.

Table 4.2

Examples of Global Interest in EQ & Leadership

Country and Population Studied	Study Results
Pakistan: Survey of 250 leaders Malik, Danish, and Munir: 2012	EQ impacts transformational leadership and organizational learning
Iran: Business leaders Ahangar: 2012	High correlations between EQ and a number of job performance variables
United Kingdom: UK project managers Clarke: 2010	EQ and "empathy" explain variances in project leaders' competencies in various soft skills
Taiwan: EQ literature review Tang, Ying, and Nelson: 2010	EQ can be conceptualized as reflecting an "ability" or a "trait"
Serbia: 308 managers Simic, Nesic, and Arsenijevic: 2012	High levels of EQ assist in lowering work stress

Clearly, EQ has established a powerful presence on the global stage. Therefore, the leader of tomorrow needs to be well versed in EQ concepts and strive to develop his or her own competencies.

How Can You Develop EQ?

Ironically, the best way to "develop" your EQ skills is an "approach" over which you have had no control. Researchers have found a powerful correlation in the effect of your having been born into a family and a culture that nurtured you in the development of your abilities of the "heart," personal awareness, and empathy.

However, regardless of your background, you can still work on your own to expand your EQ skills. Here are some examples:

Sigmar, Hynes, and Hill (2012) claim that EQ can be developed through a number of on-the-job experiences. These experiences can include intense team interactions which challenge you to develop an emotional vocabulary to use in articulating your feelings. Also, various experiential classroom activities, such as role playing, have been found to be helpful.

From a personal perspective, I have my own list of experiences and activities that I have found helpful in developing my EQ competencies. Below, I list five activities that come from experiences I have encountered throughout my experiences in leadership.

Five Easy Activities for EQ Enhancement

These five activities are "easy," meaning that you can engage in them without making a concerted effort to take off time, buy a book, or attend a seminar. As a result, they cost you nothing.

Keep a Personal Journal, Recording Your Feelings

At the end of your day, write down what emotions you are experiencing *at that specific moment in time*. Simply list them. No need to try to figure out why they are there or what is causing them. Just take an inventory of all the feelings you have at that particular moment.

The process of regularly listing your current feelings gives you practice in identifying what is taking place for you emotionally. This proficiency in self-awareness is a key component of EQ.

Sit and Observe People

As you sit in a coffee shop, observe the people at the adjacent table. As they converse, try to determine what emotions you believe each person is experiencing at that particular moment. When you come up with a guess about what each person is feeling, ask yourself what "data" you used to come up with your hypothesis. Was it the tone of voice you heard? The facial movements and expressions? Perhaps a noticeable rigidity in the person's physical posture?

This process of paying close attention to voice tone, facial movements, or the bodily posture of others offers you the chance to practice a second basic competency in all EQ models, that being your developing awareness and empathy for the feelings held by others.

Practice Making "I feel..." Statements

Pick a quiet time of day and a private location, and vocalize one "I feel..." statement after another. Do this for a few minutes. As you continue to generate these statements, you may find yourself tapping into stronger and stronger emotions.

Through this activity, you will have another opportunity to practice the EQ competency of emotional self-awareness.

Create a Day's Timeline of Experienced Emotions

At the end of a work day, as you arrive home and before you start your evening, take out a piece of paper and draw a horizontal line like the one that appears below:

_____

Use this line to represent a timeline for your day.

Then, place marks on the line that represent key events that you experienced throughout the day, such as "conflict with customer," "tense meeting with team," and "made presentation to sponsors." Your line will then have marks that may look like this:

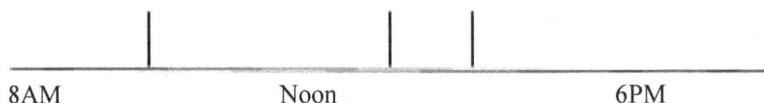

| 8AM | Noon | 6PM |

Looking at each of the perpendicular lines (which represent those key, intense events of your day), make a note about:

- What feelings you were experiencing at that moment
- What methods you used to manage those feelings

Those two sources of information—the feelings you had and how you managed them—provide you with data on how you are developing your two EQ skills of awareness of your emotions *and* your ability to moderate their expression.

Pause When Asked "How Are You Doing?"

When asked how we are doing, most of us will mechanically answer that we are "fine" or "not too bad."

Rarely do we give ourselves time to pause, seriously consider how we are *really* feeling, and then share an authentic answer with the questioner.

The next time you are asked how you are doing, pause for 5 to 10 seconds, and *really* ask yourself "Well, how *am* I doing?" Allow yourself time to identify the truthful conclusion, and then practice giving an authentic answer.

Taking time to pause like this gives you one more opportunity to practice the EQ skill of obtaining an accurate awareness of what you are feeling from moment to moment.

As you have seen in this discussion, these five exercises for enhancing your EQ are experiential and inwardly-focused, asking you to observe, reflect, and search your personal make-up at various times throughout your day.

By employing these approaches, you will find that you have many "learning opportunities" in your day. If you try these exercises on a regular basis, you will quickly gather a sense of your EQ strengths, as well as your EQ growth areas. You can then leverage your strengths to develop your weaker areas.

Some Skills Work *Here,* and Some Don't

This chapter has identified a number of distinct interpersonal communication skills and approaches you can use to enhance your effectiveness in communicating with your team and your stakeholders. I have chosen the skills of this chapter because these are my favorite skills to illustrate what you can use to be an effective interpersonal communicator.

However, it's important to acknowledge that my favorite communication skills are also reflective of who I am—a psychologist and leader whose development (both personally and professionally) has been within a Western-centric system and mindset.

Many of these skills will work well in a variety of other cultures, because the skills are philosophically grounded in efforts desired to:

- Demonstrate respect for others

- Inquire, so you can "get to know" the other person

- Acknowledge that any two project professionals, when communicating with each other, both hold inherent worth and dignity as individuals

However, as I mentioned earlier, all of these communication techniques in no way work well in all cultures.

Unfortunately, there is no standard global etiquette or guideline for the acceptance of communication skills. So, what can you do when thinking about what communications skills you should be developing for global success in the next generation?

I suggest adopting the simple yet applicable mindset of simply doing the best you can. Specifically, I encourage you to:

- Enhance the communications skills you believe to be most culturally congruent within the primary culture(s) in which you operate

- Increase your capabilities in the general competencies of emotional intelligence (EQ), as this chapter has demonstrated that EQ is a set of interpersonal competencies gaining global acceptance

And lastly, keep your eyes open to the standards and norms of other cultures. Look to see how citizens in those cultures communicate and interact.

See if you can identify patterns, as well as the rhythms and cadences within the interpersonal exchanges, and then search for nuance and subtlety.

Be an inquisitive student, and look for small openings to test your ongoing hypotheses about what communication techniques work best in which settings or cultures.

Chapter 5
Distinct Leadership Competencies:
What You Need to Succeed

Steven Flannes

The task of identifying the concrete competencies required for superior project leadership is overwhelming.

To tackle this difficult task, one could begin by examining a set of professional standards such as the PMBOK (Project Management Institute, 2008) or through reading the professional journals of the Project Management Institute and the International Project Management Association. Following these reviews, it could also be helpful to take a step or two outside the boundaries of traditional project management literature and examine the research available in the numerous journals of applied psychology and organizational development.

With such breadth of focus on leadership, one simply cannot do justice to the topic of leading project teams if one were to attempt to cover all of these sources. Therefore, in this chapter, I present a number of unique approaches to leadership, approaches that I personally value. Interestingly, despite their undeniable value, I believe that these perspectives are seldom explored in detail within traditional project management literature.

PMBOK Leadership Fundamentals:
Necessary But Not Sufficient

PMI's PMBOK is an obvious starting point for gathering a rudimentary perspective on project leadership fundamentals. In my review of PMBOK, I see a set of competencies and processes that are excellent in describing *what* needs to be done in order to achieve a successful project.

What's Missing?

What's missing, I believe, from PMBOK's various descriptions of leadership are detailed description of the specifics of leadership behavior, attitudes, and cognitions, as well as the how-to's and the steps for developing these skills.

Granted, such a description of these subtleties is not the primary purpose for a set of professional standards. Hence, one must look towards additional sources and experiences for guides in articulating the subtle skills sets needed for leading effectively within our rapidly changing global economy.

Importantly, one organization has taken the definition of leadership to more tangible and operational levels, providing business professionals from all backgrounds with a very specific, research-based set of competencies that each leader should possess to some extent. This organization is the Management Resource Group (MRG; mrg.com).

Over the years, MRG has collected leadership and assessment data from leaders representing an array of industries. Such data has led to MRG creating a model of leadership that contains five primary leadership competency groups (*Creating a vision, developing followership, implementing the vision, follow through, achieving results, and team playing)* under which twenty-two skills fall.

The MRG competencies can certainly apply to project management leaders. (For an in-depth discussion of the MRG model, as well as their various products, please see mrg.com).

However, for some leaders, the idea of trying to develop competencies in a large number of leadership skills (such as the twenty-two skills advanced by the Management Resource Group) may appear to be an overwhelming task. If so, that mindset certainly makes sense.

Such leaders may prefer a model of leadership that offers fewer distinct skills, presented more in the manner of identifying *a few core leadership functions.*

Four Leadership Hats

Such a model appears in my 2005 book, co-authored with Dr. Given Levin (Flannes and Levin, 2005). We presented four basic leadership functions that are required of the project leader. We described these functions as "hats" that the project leader wears (frequently, and often simultaneously) as he/she navigates the leadership challenges present in any one distinct period of time. These four leadership hats are presented below in Table 5.1.

Table 5.1

Four Leadership "Hats" Worn Simultaneously by All Project Leaders (Flannes and Levin, 2005)

Leadership "Hat"	Description and Ways to Develop this Leadership Skill
Leader	Being able to articulate to your team the bigger picture of how their project fits into the overall program • Work to develop the ability to tell the team "why" they are working on this project
Manager	Create the team infrastructure and organization to track the work, plus the ability to closely monitor the progress • In addition to using project management software, think about the work as a series of bundles, and create a mental dashboard for tracking milestones
Facilitator	The ability to assertively identify and pursue the resources that your team needs to succeed • Find ways to be comfortable being a "pain in the neck" to those who hold resources that you need. Never give up
Mentor	Look for opportunities, as appropriate, to subtly coach, guide, and develop your team members, even though that formal task is the job of the functional manager • Think about the mentoring that you wished you'd received earlier in your career, and then look for receptive moments to share it

This model of four leadership hats has been generally acknowledged to be both valid and efficacious in the project leadership literature. Nesbit and Martin (2011) for example, cite our four-hat model as an example of the importance for project managers in implementing well developed people skills.

Developing Trust as a Leadership Competency

Trust, like good art or an excellent restaurant, is subjectively defined by you, whenever you make an ongoing appraisal regarding "trusting someone," based upon your experiences with this person, their personal style, their belief system, or many other variables.

Through my work as a psychologist and a leader, I have found that when a team member says that he or she "trusts the project leader," the team member is referring to various combinations of four beliefs and behaviors.

These attributes include: acting in good faith, being authentic, demonstrating congruence and a reciprocal approach to relationships, and personal consistency. Below, you will find fictitious statements that exemplify each of these four attributes:

1. "The leader treats me in a way that suggests they have my best interests in mind, even when I don't get everything I want on a project."

    -   The leader described above is acting in *good faith*, treating others with the best of intentions, and is not working surreptitiously against the interests of any team member.

    -   This leader is also demonstrating *authenticity,* which suggests an appropriate openness or interpersonal transparency.

2. "When my team leader makes a statement or commitment, I believe she will follow through on that commitment."

    -   In this example, the leader is demonstrating *congruence* between what they *say* and what they actually *do*. This is very, very important.

3. "Our project leader treats me in a manner that is respectful and is suggestive of a basic human equality, even if there is a power differential in the relationship."

    -   Here, this leader is demonstrating a relationship that is *reciprocal* in nature, in which general courtesies and a "treating-others-as equals" mindset exist.

4. "Regardless of whether or not I like the style of my leader, I still perceive a core consistency in his behavior across situations, providing me with some sense of predictability as to what to expect from him over time."

    -   This leader is demonstrating a *personal consistency and continuity,* whereby team members have knowledge of how he "ticks." Such a leader does not display large fluctuations in behavior, or changes in his emotional presentation of self.

These four leader attributes and behaviors are presented in summary form in Table 5.2 below.

Table 5.2

Leadership Attributes that Assist in Building Trust

Leader Attribute	Example	Trust-Building Benefit
Good faith efforts presented authentically	Regardless of the situation, treats others with an inherent consideration of their well-being	Individuals work harder when they believe they are working for someone who has their general well-being in mind
Congruence of words/actions	When a leader makes a commitment, she delivers, or tells stakeholders why she cannot	Leader congruence creates a "believability" factor for team members, which increases team member motivation
Relationship reciprocity	Leader approaches others as equals, seeking opinions, displaying respect	Leader's reciprocal behavior creates a tight bond/working connection with team members
Consistency of behavior	In good times and bad, leader's behavior and emotions are fairly consistent, with few big mood or behavior swings	Leader consistency, in both behavior and mood, often creates a sense of "safety" for team members, allowing them to focus on tasks, and not on the possible behavioral eruptions of the leader

Leadership Research:
What Skills Are Being Identified?

The previous section described some fundamental project leadership skills I find to be important. These skills are *required, but are not sufficient* for exemplary project leadership. The following section describes additional skills that you will need, skills that are being presented in the literature on leadership. Please consider the following works.

An excellent piece of research on the topic of the impact upon performance of project manager leadership style is the work of Turner and Muller (Project Management Journal, 2005). Turner and Muller do an exceptional job of presenting the reader with a detailed history of leadership theory, as well as articulating the importance of a leader's Emotional Intelligence (EQ). This article, in my opinion, is a must-read for project professionals desiring to gain a valuable perspective on the evolution of project leadership competencies.

In recent years, several other researchers have also examined the impact of personality and leadership competencies upon the success of the project leader.

For example, other writers have surveyed the perceptions of IT executives on desired interpersonal leadership competencies. Their research found six critical core competencies, and of these six, five had the soft skills variable of "communication." in common. Such results are interesting, suggesting that IT executives may assume that many IT professionals hold basic technical competencies, but the true "keepers" would appear to be those IT professionals displaying the added value of skill in the soft skills.

Leadership skills may also be viewed from a national perspective. Steers, Sanchez-Runde, and Nardon (2012) looked at leadership skills in terms of what type of leadership style is preferred in various countries. They report that such research has traditionally found consistent patterns with regard to style preferences. Their results are excerpted below:

Russia, United States:	Assertive and visible leadership is preferred
Norway, Japan:	Leaders prefer to work behind the scenes
Mexico, Spain:	A desire for high profile, respect—commanding
Laos, Malaysia:	Humble, lower-profile leaders are preferred

Such research on country-based leadership preferences is helpful for us in thinking through our best practices in cross-cultural settings. However, as I have stated previously, it is also important to avoid over generalizing such descriptions, and to not "objectify" the citizens of a particular country as having fixed and static preferences. For me, the challenge is to gingerly balance an appreciation for the uniqueness of the respective culture with keeping in mind that each person from the said culture also holds unique preferences and desires.

"Positive" Leadership

In recent years, "positive" psychology has been in the public's awareness. Because of the word "positive," this branch of psychology, and in our case "positive" leadership, can easily be dismissed as overly simplistic, stressing a "put on a happy face" injunction that one should adopt.

Fortunately, researchers like Youseff and Luthans (2012) present a more sophisticated and nuanced description of the varying aspects of positive leadership. To do so, they highlight the term "positive global leadership," stating that it involves four attitudinal states, including: the ability to create the perception of "hope," promoting the belief that team members have the ability to impact their environment, resilience (see Chapter 7 for a detailed discussion of resilience), and optimism regarding future events.

Personally, I believe that for a leader wanting to display such positive leadership attributes, he or she would have to adopt a number of mindsets and behaviors. These behaviors would include the ability to:

- Create a realistic but optimistic team attitude from the start of the project

- Help team members identify their strengths, and encourage their empowerment by not limiting their self-direction and innovation

There is one special point in the work of Youseff and Luthans that I find to be especially important when thinking about positive leadership. This point is the concept that positive leadership is *not simply the absence of negative leadership*. In fact, it is a leadership style noted for the initiation of various proactive, positive behaviors. So, it requires positive action, not just a reduction in negative actions.

Having just described the concepts of negative and positive leadership, I want to add a cautionary note about too quickly adopting these two concepts as independent concepts. I must say that there can be a risk in adopting firm boundaries between negative and positive leadership behaviors.

Here is the risk: When such concepts are taken too concretely, there emerges a tendency to feel as though one needs to somehow jump a chasm from exhibiting "negative" behaviors to exhibiting "positive" behaviors. When behavior change is framed in such absolutes, there is often a resulting lack of motivation in trying a new behavior, due to a concern that one might not do it the "right way."

Instead, there is the highly practical virtue in viewing "negative" and "positive" as the extreme points along a linear continuum.

Such a *continuum approach to behavior change* facilitates one's getting into the mindset of taking small steps, progressing along the continuum, in an iterative manner. Below is an example of this iterative mindset for behavior change:

- Methodically adding a single lap around the track each week in my running program, instead of focusing on going from being "out of shape" to being "in shape"

As with all behavior change, a small-step approach (i.e., pursuing gradual changes) reduces the risk of making no change at all, due to the possible hindrance of all-or-none thinking.

Global Leadership

Holt and Seki (2012) co-authored an important article on the subject of global leadership. In it, they comment that previous leadership trends all too often define global leadership in an excessively Western-centric manner. Holt and Seki, however, provide a strong case for the idea that new models of global leadership need to be more, in my words, conceptually inclusive, given the global economic trends that create a "flatter" world.

In discussing this idea of a less Western-centric leadership model, Holt and Seki identify a number of elements present in successful global leadership. From my perspective as a practicing psychologist, I find two elements to be particularly important: the ability to manage paradoxes, and one's comfort with the personal posture of "being." The importance of each element is outlined below.

Managing Paradoxes

While I find one's ability to manage paradoxes to be one of the most important interpersonal leadership skills, it is also, in my opinion, inadequately emphasized in the world of project leadership. So, here are my thoughts on the importance of managing paradox.

A theoretical given in working cross-culturally is that by definition, you are bringing your cultural heritage into the world of another, and are therefore bound to experience a cultural paradox. Though you may try, you simply cannot avoid this, nor should you, as the ability to leverage such differences is a desired quality that can serve you well.

From a psychological perspective, your ability to manage paradox is a function of how well you can simultaneously "hold," in a cognitive sense, two fundamentally opposing views of the same situation.

To simultaneously hold these contradictory views, you must be comfortable with:

- Dwelling in a period where no clear action path is evident, and managing the anxiety that such situations create

- Looking for the value present in each opposite view

- Not letting your anxiety "force" you to quickly pick which of the two opposites you believe is the "right one"

- Gradually accepting that the world in which you live is filled with such paradoxes, and that you are not doing anything wrong when you notice that you are not able to decide which one is the "right one"

This process of comfortably holding two opposite views of the same situation is challenging. In essence, you are asking yourself to jump from your familiar mindset into an unfamiliar one, holding the faith that within this unknown, you will be able to find alternative truths and legitimacies that you simply cannot identify ahead of time.

In many ways, this process really does involve undertaking an act of faith, in which you are asking yourself to trust that different approaches to the same problem can be just as valid and efficacious as your tried-and-true approach to the problem. In the next section, I present one possible example of trying to "hold" such dual perspectives.

Laos and Russia: Is There a Third Way?

Below is an example of this psychologically sophisticated process of holding two disparate views of the same situation simultaneously, able to understand that each has its own value, benefit, and efficacy. As you will see, my example is both concrete and overly simplified.

If you recall earlier in this chapter, I offered comments regarding the preferred leadership styles found in various countries. One finding suggested that Russians prefer an active and visible leader, while citizens of Laos prefer a leader who is humble and who carries a lower profile. Assume the veracity of those finding as you consider the following fictitious example:

> A project leader from Laos was working in Russia, leading a project team addressing a complex task. So, how does this leader from Laos then decide what the "right" way is to lead when based in Moscow? Should he use the Laotian perspective? The Russian perspective? Or perhaps something else?

What this leader should do is hold both cultural mindsets, looking for means of identifying an additional way, or path, one that is more than just a compromise between the two cultural forces, or an additive total of both approaches.

Such a mindset requires an interactive and iterative process, searching for commonalities, while simultaneously framing differences as opportunities to create a new, innovative way to proceed.

This leader must be able to comfortably shift her perspective back and forth from the macro level to the micro level, reframing her personal discomfort or anxiety as a natural reaction, trusting that over time she will feel more comfortable dwelling between the two worlds.

Ultimately, she will see that her challenge involves a shift to a mindset noted for perceiving differences as *valued counterpoints* in the process of leveraging such differences to develop innovative approaches that drive creative solutions and products.

Develop Comfort with "Just Being"

I have found that one particularly crucial skill for a leader to develop is the ability of *being present.* To do so, you need to be able to convey to the other party the experience that you, as team leader, are in fact really "there" when communicating with them. "Being there" involves:

- A nonjudgmental attention to what the other person is saying

- An ability to clear your mind of other topics and cognitive streams, actively listening to the person

- A body language (noted by focused eye contact and a forward-leaning posture) that communicates focus and immediate engagement

Much of the current literature on the psychological sophistication required of today's leader speaks to the importance of *being present*, citing the benefits of displaying such a focused interpersonal sense of immediacy.

For example, I am functioning in my *being mode* when I am not operating in an objectified definition of myself. Such an objectified definition of me, for example, could be "California psychologist," "Margaret's nephew," or "project management writer."

While such titles or descriptions of me are certainly accurate at the micro level, they do not embrace the breadth of who I am. When I am "being," I am responding to the world from the essence of *who I am*, as compared to *what I am*.

Below is a scenario that illustrates functioning in the being present mode:

> Imagine you are in a foreign country, having dinner with "a friend of a friend." While this person may be someone you have heard of, you have little knowledge of his career or his personal life.

> Both of you are uncomfortable in speaking each other's native tongue, and as a result, the conversation is minimal. (Communication takes place primarily by the two of you pointing at objects, offering hand gestures and smiles in service of delivering your message).

Since you are the "visitor," you have almost no knowledge about the details of the dining experience: what food will be served, proper dining etiquette, the names of the dishes to be enjoyed, the length of this meal, and the custom for who pays for such a meal in this friend-of-a-friend pairing.

To get through an evening like this comfortably, you might try the following:

- Relate on the most basic of levels, letting go of trying to ascertain the work that each of you perform, or the titles you hold

- You let go of expectations regarding how the evening should proceed, reminding yourself to "let the evening come to you"

Thus, you function without title, content knowledge, or a goal-directed purpose. Nor do you even consider trying to guide the process of the evening. You let things come to you, and trust that you will respond accordingly.

So, during this evening, you are successfully functioning in the dimension of "being present."

Working with Cognitive Complexity through Self-Reflection

Dragoni and McAlpine (2012) stress that global leaders must also obtain expertise in the area of handling cognitive complexity.

They posit that three distinct forces contribute to the presence of cognitive complexity. These forces are as follows: the factors of multiplicity (where the leader must contend with large samples of political systems, customers, and competitors), enterprise interdependency, and a pervasive ambiguity about how leaders must make decisions in cross-national settings.

Dragoni and McAlpine speak of the benefits of reflecting on your cross-cultural experiences. Such reflection can help you integrate your experience of complexity from new settings such as those experienced via cross-cultural immersion.

This self-reflection process happens after you have been immersed in a setting in which competing cultural practices have cognitively pulled you in different directions.

As a psychologist, when I explore ways to use self-reflection to process contrasting, complex experiences, I think of the following:

- To self-reflect, you need to seek a quiet setting where you can review what you just recently experienced in that unique setting, looking for both differences and commonalities. You should reflect on what you learned about *you*, regarding personal variables such as your cognitions, anxieties, and your decision making process in this novel setting.

Below, I offer two vignettes that illustrate the process and benefits of self-reflecting on any cross-cultural immersion experience that you might experience.

First Vignette

Imagine you are in the airport, waiting to board your flight home following your vacation to a country that you've not visited before.

As you sit, you find yourself thinning out the papers in your backpack. As you go through each piece of paper, deciding whether or not you would like to keep that hotel receipt or museum guide, you find yourself re-living many parts of the trip.

In doing so, experiences and memories float to mind, both positive and negative. As these thoughts surface, you may notice that these experiences "changed" you in some way. Possibly, you "learned" (in quotation marks because you already knew this idea before, but not on an experiential level) that peoples' views on what is important in life *really are different,* or that you had brought with you many cultural value judgments to your two week stay. So, as your reflection continues, you may find yourself learning more and more about *you* as a person.

Second Vignette

The second vignette illustrates that your self-reflection should not be not limited to a one time "debriefing" of what you learned about yourself.

Imagine that you have been home from the above described trip for a number of days, having put jet lag behind you, and have returned to work.

One Saturday morning, you decide to do some editing of the 1,493 digital photos you took on the trip. As you scroll through the photos, your editing and cropping gets delayed every so often as you come across a photo that reminds you of an intense, meaningful experience you had, one that left you with important lessons learned about your own cultural competencies or beliefs. You might notice that memories surface *then* that did not surface at the airport.

These two vignettes suggest to me that you will learn more about yourself if you make it a habit to regularly self-reflect on important events and experiences in your life. In many ways, this process is similar to that of psychotherapy, in which the client may reflect on a single situation or event a number of times, each time learning more about themselves.

If I were to offer a checklist representation of this process of reflecting on complex cultural experiences, integrating your lessons learned from such self-reflection, I would offer the 5-step process below.

1. Immerse yourself in a different culture

2. Reflect on observed culture clashes

3. Attempt to integrate the complexities, and then create new "mental maps" of yourself and your world

4. Use new mental maps to guide new experiences

5. Continually repeat these steps as needed

As you engage in this ongoing self-reflection process, be sure to note the benefits that come to you. Among other things, you will find that it helps in forming new views of yourself and the world, views that are further enhanced, modified, or changed by repeated *iterations.*

Leader Success through *Encoding* and *Decoding*

The conceptual makeup of encoding and decoding relates to the communication process. *Encoding* involves the range of internal processes you experience whilst transforming your inner thoughts and feelings into messages that you can then use to communicate with others. *Decoding,* on the other hand, relates to your taking the encoded messages of others, and transferring the symbols within those messages into codes and concepts (ideas) that have meaning for you.

Even though the encoding-decoding process is quite basic in theory, it still is an important process nevertheless, and when poorly executed by either party, an environment is created in which inadequate communicative tendencies flourish. The following situations serve as examples of these problematic scenarios:

- The leader's message uses symbols not fully understood by a fellow team member

- The team member, due to his or her own *cognitive distractibility*, and/or personal biases, decodes only a portion of the leader's message

Henderson (2004) studied the impact of a project manager's encoding abilities, and came to two conclusions. First, he discovered that the level of team performance is significantly connected to the project manager's *encoding* competencies. Secondly, he ascertained that the level of team satisfaction is significantly associated with the project manager's combined skills in *encoding* and *decoding.*

Thus, it becomes apparent that the give (encoding) and take (decoding) of effective leader-team communication results in team members experiencing the highest levels of satisfaction. And this makes sense.

I like to think of the leader's encoding process as a communication effort in which the leader focuses not just on what he or she *wishes to say* (as it is a given that she will be undoubtedly "saying something"), but rather, focuses on what information he or she *wants to transfer* to the other party. Specifically, I have found a number of benefits to focusing on what information *I intend to transfer*: Some of these benefits are listed below:

- Focusing on transferring *information* helps avoid getting stuck in the transferring of *emotion*

- Creating a more tangible and purposive nature to your communications lowers your risk of others perceiving you are simply "talking about the subject"

- The act of transferring information creates an action-oriented mindset for all parties involved, as it carries this implied question: "Now that I have this information, what should *I* do with it?"

Become an "Ambidextrous" Leader

Probst, Raisch, and Tushman (2011) encourage flexible leadership through the act of your being "ambidextrous."

These writers suggest that the ambidextrous leader not only executes the processes of the existing business successfully, but also implements a strategic capability to establish new growth initiatives. Hence, doing two things at once.

Ambidextrous leadership thus involves managing different mindsets. One such mindset (the one for managing the existing business) appears to suggest an enterprise-inward focus on operations, looking at issues of quality, margin, and production. The leadership focus on new business, on the other hand, appears to suggest a mindset of a market gap analysis, economic trends, and opportunities in product innovation.

Clearly, one person *can* discharge both types of leadership, but many leaders cannot.

When exploring the best ways to develop this type of leadership competency, I emphasize again the profound benefits of experiential learning. As I mentioned earlier, significant personal changes *do not* happen easily when the learning medium is highly didactic or content based (such as classes, books, or recorded presentations).

Rather, the most effective vehicles for learning and personal development are those delivered individually (such as executive coaching), or experientially (ongoing seminars with fixed participants). My thoughts on why I find experiential learning to be so important for developing psychologically sophisticated leadership capabilities are presented below:

Immerse Yourself in Different Cultures (Travel, Exchanges, Business, etc.)

- Heightens your awareness of the paradox that all cultures are simultaneously *similar* and *divergent* in relation to your culture of origin

Engage in Ongoing Seminars or Trainings with a Fixed Number of the Same, Recurring Participants

- The continuity of ongoing growth experiences with the same people offers you a potent medium for making changes

Consider the Resource of One-to-One Personal Coaching

- Working intimately with a personal coach provides a setting in which tailored goals can be identified for you based upon *what you need or want.* Additionally, such a setting has an interpersonal accountability that aids increased development and action

So, as you look to expand your sophisticated leader competencies, seek out the experiential mediums, allowing you to work on these skills in a more intimate and powerful setting.

An Overview of This Chapter's Skills and Competencies

In this chapter, I have selected an assortment of leadership skills, competencies, and attributes based upon my view of important areas often lacking adequate attention in the publications of mainstream project leadership.

Much of this selected material is heavily grounded in my experience in leading groups and my work as a psychologist. Hopefully, the areas and work I have selected for you will open doors to ideas you may not have previously considered.

An overview of the all skills and competencies introduced in this chapter can be found in Table 5.3.

Table 5.3

Overview of Distinct Leadership Skills and Competencies

Skill or Competency	Author	Example
PMBOK: leader descriptions	Project Management Institute, 2008	Basic guidelines about leadership functions
22 research-based leadership competencies	Management Resource Group (mrg.com)	22 skills covering four basic leadership functions
Your simultaneously wearing four different leadership "hats"	Flannes and Levin, 2005	Leader, Manager, Facilitator, and Coach
Developing trust with your team members	Flannes (personal views)	Good faith efforts, authenticity, congruence, and reciprocal relationships
IT function soft skills that center on communication	Stevenson and Starkweather, 2010	Verbal and written communication skills, as well as comfort with ambiguity
Awareness of country-specific leadership style preferences	Steer, Sanchez-Runde, and Nardon, 2012	Russia and U.S. described as preferring assertive and visible leaders
Maintain a distinction between "negative" and "positive" leadership	Youssef and Luthans, 2012	These forms of leadership are not just end points on the same continuum
Develop "global leadership" skills	Holt and Seki, 2012	Multicultural effectiveness and managing paradoxes
Handle cognitive complexity	Dragoni and McAlpine, 2012	Develop comfort and skill in handling ambiguity, multiplicity, and interdependence
Engage in "self-reflection of experiences"	Dragoni and McAlpine, 2012	Following cross-cultural experiences, reflect upon what you learned about *you*
Develop skills in encoding and decoding	Henderson, 2004	Communicate clearly, and listen effectively
Become an "ambidextrous" leader	Probst, Raisch, and Tushman, (2011)	Be skillful in effectively managing the current business *and* in developing new opportunities

Continuing to Develop Your Leadership Skills

The field of leadership study and research is incredibly broad, with rapid changes taking place in the definition of what constitutes "global leadership." As I mentioned at the beginning of this chapter, I find it hard to know how to approach all of the available information.

However, below is a four-step process or mindset that I recommend. These steps can assist you in developing your leadership skills through a natural progression. Throughout my work in this field, I have found the process below to be extremely helpful in your deciding "where to start," and how to proceed when looking to develop your leadership skills.

- Start with the PMBOK, and develop a grounding of what you think you do well, and then identify your growth areas.

- Look at the leadership competencies presented in any comprehensive, skill-based leadership model. Such a system takes your search to a deeper and more meaningful level than exists within PMBOK. Identify both your strong points and your weaknesses.

- Begin an informal, ongoing look at "global leadership" research trends. This review will keep your outlook current.

- And finally, become comfortable with the idea that leadership beliefs are like fashion: they will constantly be changing, but some core elements will retain value over time. Become grounded in what works for you, and then add to your list any meaningful new competencies that you come across.

Above all, identify some specific goals, and proceed in small steps. Stay away from the mindset of trying to do it "right." Experiment. Take some chances. Steal ideas and approaches from others.

As with any personal developmental goal, leverage your current leadership strengths to develop new strengths. Focus on growing as an individual, as such personal growth gives you expanded capabilities for your day job as a leader.

Chapter 6
Achieving and Maintaining
High Levels of Performance

Steven Flannes

Achieving high levels of individual and team performance is one thing. Maintaining those high levels during difficult times is another thing completely. Consequently, I have two goals for this chapter:

1. Describe a set of leadership performance enhancing practices that you can follow towards performing at the top of your game

And because it is an unpredictable world out there, with risk factors constantly in play, the second goal of this chapter is to:

2. Describe a number of active initiatives that you can use to assist yourself and your team in returning to high levels of performance following some form of project or individual crisis

Achieving High Levels of Leader Performance

When I think of what I can do to get myself functioning at my highest levels, I can turn to the many approaches that we have all heard about before. The list of these types of activities includes getting exercise, watching my diet, getting plenty of rest, maybe finding a mentor, selective reading, and seeking work-life balance.

All of these are valuable resources, but in this chapter let us consider some approaches that I believe are more powerful. And as you will see, these resources are not just project management specific, but are drawn from a wide range of fields. Hopefully, you will see a resource here that you have not considered before.

In the first section of this chapter, I present three unique approaches for performance enhancement, and these include practices from the world of sports psychology, positive psychology, and your immersion in *flow* activities.

Three Unique Perspectives

I believe these approaches offer unique and powerful development avenues that are not available from traditional approaches. Personally, in my dual career as psychologist/leader, I have many times witnessed the efficacy of these different approaches.

You will find that these approaches are not project management specific. Please consider that this fact ironically may be a significant asset.

So, as you read these upcoming sections, your challenge is to take the ideas and apply them directly to your own situation, whether that be in your role as project team member, project manager, program manager, portfolio manager, or "other."

Sports Psychology: Contributions to Performance Enhancement

Let me make the case that the world of sports psychology has much to offer those who want to perform at their best in the world of project management. Below, I present two areas emanating from sports psychology that can be easily applied, I believe, to your goal of achieving high levels of performance.

The first approach from sports psychology is that of visualization. For example, to perform well in tennis, you might be coached by a sports psychologist to visualize how you want to display your skills when in actual competition:

- You would be encouraged to "see," in your mind's eye, how you want to approach the ball, how you want to begin your swing, and how you desire to complete your follow through.

- You would also be encouraged to visualize how you would subjectively want to feel as you performed the physical tasks.

This process of visualization, in which you call up the ideal physical behaviors and mental attitudes, happens in the quiet moments of mental practice before a tennis match. You can also use this technique when you are focusing on improving your performance within the project management arena.

For example, if you have struggled over the years with feeling anxious when leading a meeting, you could try visualizing how you would prefer to feel. For example, let's say you desire to feel more confident and articulate in the meeting, and also feel less anxious. Table 6.1 shows how you can apply the visualization process towards those goals.

Table 6.1

Applying Visualization to Goals

Desired Behavior or Feeling State When Presenting to a Meeting	Definition of Desired Behavior or Feeling State You Want to Have in the Meeting	Create a "Visualization Script" to Repeat to Self in Quiet Moments Before the Meeting
"I want to feel more *confident* when I make a presentation"	I make a statement, and then move forward with my talk I see questions as opportunities, and not as challenges	"I am standing tall in front of the group. I make a statement knowing that I've done more work on the topic than others in the room. I hear my voice being strong and purposive as my words leave my mouth."
"I want to also feel *less anxious* when I'm presenting"	I view questions as an opportunity to interact, not as a call to defend something I said	"I see myself using active listening to restate what the person is asking. I see myself nodding as they speak. I see myself taking as much time as I need before I answer."

Visualizing these self-crafted scripts, in the quiet moments before key events, provides a positive road map to follow once you are on the stage. Thus, when you are on stage, your goal is then one of implementing your vision, letting yourself "be as you want to be."

Obviously, this is a simplified treatment of goals that are often more complicated. However, visualization, done on a regular basis, is a great place to start.

A related approach that I very much like from the world of sports psychology is for you to focus on the *behavior*, and not on the *outcome* This approach seems to encompass a variety of ideas from numerous wisdom traditions. Such ideas can include:

- Don't get too far ahead of yourself

- Take one step at a time

- Live in the moment; that's all you really have, anyway

A benefit of focusing on the behavior you want to execute (such as "confidently speaking up in a meeting"), as compared to the outcome, is the idea that you will be creating less performance anxiety for yourself. Here is how that works:

- Rather than have two goals—executing a new behavior *and* being concerned with whether or not the behavior creates a desired outcome—you focus on just one goal—that being executing the new behavior (and letting the outcome take care of itself).

Personally, much of the appeal for me of these contributions from sports psychology is their simplicity. Additionally, most of us already have some experience in using these approaches (such as visualization and focusing on the behavior) to other activities in life we were attempting to master (such as dancing or skiing).

Positive Psychology

The field of positive psychology is a meld of a number of different legacies and approaches.

For me, the field ranges from the autobiographical observations of what cognitive approaches people used to survive in concentration camps during World War II (Frankl, 1958) to recent developments in the field of resilience (Seligman, 2011), which are being applied to how can people best recover from a devastating crisis or loss. (Resilience will be discussed in detail later in this chapter).

Chronologically located somewhere between Frankl and resilience is the field of cognitive behavioral psychology. Cognitive psychology takes a very practical and applied approach towards identifying tools that you can use to function at your optimal level (Isett and Isett, 2010, and Burns, 1999).

Two performance enhancement approaches that come from the world of cognitive behavioral practices are the application the "control/no control" exercise and the crafting of a "neutral cognition."

Control/No Control Exercise

Here is the benefit of applying a "control/no control" exercise.

Assume you are facing a difficult leadership situation, and you need to perform the best you can in order to facilitate a solution. The control/no control exercise helps you focus on what you have control over, *and* also what you do not have control over. Thus, with this knowledge, you focus your energy on "what you have control over" and let go of focusing your attention and energy on "what you have no control over."

Specifically, to illustrate this resource, assume that you face the following leadership problem: I need to perform at my highest levels because I'm being assigned to try to recover a failing (but program-critical) project in a country that I know nothing about. Therefore, in using the control/no control exercise, you would make two ongoing lists of:

- Aspects of the situation over which you can exert *some control*, and

- Aspects of the situation of which you have *no control*

These two lists might look like the following:

Table 6.2

Control and No-Control Variables

Aspects of Situation I Have Some Control Over	Aspects of Situation I Have No Control Over
Contact a colleague who might have some knowledge of the culture	Developing mastery of the cultural practices of that country before I travel
Attempt to transfer current projects to a colleague	Whether or not anyone else will take over these projects
Speak with sponsoring executive about the appropriateness of modifying the scope of the troubled project	Political considerations that may or may not impact my desire to modify the project scope
Quickly review project and see if I think I need additional resources, ask for what I want	Whether or not anyone will agree to fund my requests
Saying "no" to neighbor who wants me to join him this week as a youth baseball coach	The level of irritation my neighbor will have when I say "no" to him about coaching
Pack my workout clothes with the hope of continuing my exercise program	Whether or not the hotel where I'll be staying has workout facilities
Initiating discussion with my functional manager about my requests for resuming my position when I return	Whether or not the functional manager wants to honor my request, or even if she has the power to do so

And as you can also see, the items on the list involve some of obvious significance (scope of the project) and some of less obvious importance (my hopes for exercise capability).

Include both types of items on your list, because such breadth of items will do nothing but assist you in functioning at your very best. Almost nothing is too insignificant to include on your list.

Such a listing allows you to focus your attention, energies, and abilities on the items on the left side of the chart, thus increasing your chances for achieving optimal performance. For me, the key idea here is expressed in the following question:

- Why tie up your resources and energies by attending to variables over which you have no control?

Craft a Neutral Cognition

The second cognitive tool that I believe helps you perform at your highest level is the process by which you take a troubling situation, requiring your best, and you then look to craft a "neutral self-talk" statement regarding the situation.

The underlying idea here is that you may hinder your performance should you allow the ongoing repetition of negative self-talk. Negative self-talk usually limits your willingness to act. Additionally, negative self-talk ends up lowering your expectations around the performance level you believe you can achieve.

Using the example from above involving the project recovery effort within a new culture, a natural, but *negative* self-talk statement might be:

"I don't think I have much of a chance to save this project. The quality of the work has been poor, and I know nothing at all about the culture."

Creating a more neutral self-talk statement (but one that is still grounded in the difficult reality of the situation), I might try saying this to myself:

"While this looks really tough right now, I'll take it one day at a time when I get there, and just maybe I'll run across some positive aspects of the project that I haven't seen so far."

This neutral self-talk can really help you perform at your best. When you are employing neutral self-talk, you are accurately acknowledging the difficulty you face, but you are also staying open to new possibilities.

In summary, this method of creating a neutral cognition for performing at your highest levels asks you to:

1. Be realistic, and do not deny the difficulties that you face

2. Do not close the door to *the possibility* of unexpected good news or new avenues for problem solving

Get Involved in Your Own *Flow* Activities

Becoming involved in your own *flow* activities is an excellent method to use towards assisting you in performing at your best by providing you with intellectual, emotional, and spiritual fulfillment.

"Flow" (Csikszentmihalyi, 2008) is a very interesting concept that has been applied to the areas of creativity and personal wellness. I also see it as a powerful tool, or practice, for leaders to be involved with in order to be intellectually and emotional nurtured through immersion in what one knows to be his or her own *flow* activities.

Flow activities are those activities that help you feel recharged, and also better about yourself in particular, and the world in general. Nakamura and Csikszentmihalyi (2009) describe flow activities as consisting of experiences where:

- You are intensely immersed in a task or experience that you enjoy

- You have the required skills needed for the task

- You lose a sense of time and self-consciousness when involved in the activity

- The activity is intrinsically rewarding, and you often conclude the experience with a renewed self of personal well-being

As I have discovered over the years, flow activities can be almost anything. During the seminars I have presented in a number of countries over the years, project management professionals have shared the following activities and experiences with me as examples of their own flow activities:

- Playing a musical instrument, reading, or attending an arts performance

- Cooking at the urban homeless shelter

- Woodworking

- Organizing the home office of a friend, having been given permission to throw things away

- Hand-plowing a small field after the first rains of spring

- Building and repairing fences on a small, family-owned winery

- Running and many forms of exercise

- Time spent with their children or pets (not necessarily in that order)

- Sitting or walking in nature

Clearly, flow activities are defined in the eye of the beholder.

I have found that regular immersion in my own flow activities (running, reading, fishing, sitting quietly, and being in nature) gives me the following performance enhancing benefits:

- I feel more vital, alive, and powerful, and have a more optimistic outlook

- I am more willing to take action, or try something new

- I experience a greater confidence that things will work out

It's also my experience that involvement with flow activities helps one return to high levels of performance after having experienced a stressful event or problem. Consider the following comments on flow as a stress management strategy:

I mentioned that I have included flow activities in my people skills seminars over the years. In the seminar, there is a section where I discuss managing your stress so that you can perform at your best. Over the years, I have asked hundreds of project professionals to state which approach (of four I present to them) is *their favorite approach for managing stress*. Almost always, flow is easily selected as the number one choice. No other approach even comes close for these groups.

Why would that be? Here is my speculation on why project professionals choose flow activities as their preferred tool for handling stress:

- Project managers, by definition, like to be involved with tangible activities (projects) in which they can immerse themselves in the process (project scope and project stages).

- Flow activities offer knowledge workers (like project professionals) an opportunity to temporarily turn down their level of professional involvement in the world, and become involved experientially in an enjoyable activity.

Variables that *Hinder* Your Performance

Up to this point in the chapter, I have presented an assortment of techniques and approaches that I have found assist me and others in performing at high levels.

Now, the chapter will approach the topic of high performance from a different angle—that angle being how one can perform well, given that the world is fraught with uncertainty.

Briefly, I present below an overview of variables that can hinder high levels of project performance. Starting from a high elevation view, I present the subjects of complexity dynamics and uncertainty as forces that may hinder performance levels for individuals as well as teams.

Complexity and Uncertainty

Folke (2010) presents the idea that almost all systems are constantly in flux, operating in unpredictable and non-linear ways.

The idea that systems operate in non-linear ways seems to challenge an unspoken cognitive map followed by many of us in project management: that belief being that project scope, specifications, and schedule can create a linear world in which we can achieve high levels of performance by "following the plan."

However, I believe that if we are too embracing of a linear perspective, we are in jeopardy of taking too much at face value, and therefore being at risk for lowered performance, should the non-linear complexity of the system emerge when we do not expect it.

Related in espousing the belief that systems and events are far more unpredictable than the bulk of us would like to acknowledge is Taleb (2007), who stresses that unpredictable and rare events can have huge impacts on a system. Taleb's view is that we cannot plan for the emergence of these events (hence our "risk management" efforts may be limited in effectiveness). He believes that since we cannot control these events, we should do what we can to develop a robust ability to respond to them, and take advantage of them, when they do occur.

So, what do these views of uncertainty and complexity say to me in terms of my goal in this chapter of focusing on ways of achieving and maintaining high levels of performance? I believe that such work tells us that:

- Unseen variables and forces are continually operating and re-organizing within the systems (projects) in which we operate

- To achieve high levels of performance given such uncertainty, we need to focus on developing a robust resilience to these emerging, often disruptive events, as compared to investing too heavily in risk management strategies that may be out of date before they are implemented

Information Overload and Multitasking

Huge amounts of data are available to you as you complete your work. Consequently, you are faced with the idea that multitasking is a necessary evil. However, be cautious in too completely embracing multitasking, as I describe its pitfalls in the following sections.

Begley (2011) presents work done in the area of information overload. She offers brain-based research that notes that while there can be a decision-making benefit to increasing the load of information presented to an individual, at some point continuing to increase the level of information results in a decrease in the effectiveness of decision making.

Multitasking: Can You Tame It?

As I mentioned, multitasking is a necessary evil. However, please keep in mind that it is not necessarily the most effective approach to working. Consider this idea:

- Just because you are simultaneously working on lots of things does not mean that you are getting lots of things done.

Here is why that paradox exists:

Researchers have found that there are "switching costs" when you quickly move from one topic to another, and then back again (American Psychological Association, 2006). Switching costs is a negative consequence to multitasking, such as a loss of time efficiency, and a possible diminished level of work quality, especially when working on complex tasks.

These inefficiencies come from what has been termed "goal shifting" (when you make a conscious decision to shift your work focus from task A to task B). Additionally, efficiency is hampered by a cognitive "warm up" period where you have to get reacquainted with the details, goals, or issues of the next task.

To manage the risk of "switching costs" when multitasking, remember the following:

- Do not assume that you are working effectively just because you are multitasking (due to the concept of switching costs)

- For tasks requiring attention to complex variables, try to avoid working on those situations while multitasking

The risks arising from task "switching" are also addressed by a number of writers who suggest that, as much as possible, one should minimize the allocation of one individual to numerous, simultaneous projects, and when one individual is involved with one project, or one task, do as much as possible to reduce interruptions of either a cognitive or interpersonal nature.

I'd like to offer a brief comment before I leave this discussion of information overload and the necessity of multitasking. I believe that it is easy to fall into the mindset that says "there is just too much information that I have to look at" and therefore "multitasking is just a way of life now."

The ideas cited above suggest there are personal strategies you can try in order to reduce the negative impact of multitasking. I therefore believe that your role as leader requires you to try these approaches, while also modeling them for your team.

The Negative Influence of Certain Personality Attributes

Personality attributes can obviously help or hamper leader performance. Let's talk about the personal styles, cognitions, and behaviors that can hinder performance.

One particular personality attribute that warrants discussion is Type A behavior (Rosenmann and Friedman, 1977). Type A behavior consists of behavior and attitudes that can create unease, self-criticism, and in some cases, a lack of action. Type A behavior is often viewed as involving:

- A quest for perfectionism (regardless of the importance of the task)

- A sense of time urgency, wanting a task to be completed as soon as possible (even when not logically necessary)

- A personal style often noted for chronic irritation, crabbiness, and self-criticism

Many researchers view Type A personality as a free-standing condition. However, I prefer to think of it as a way of relating to the world that all of us can fall into from time to time. Such a view gives us more flexibility, and does not require that we self-select into, or out of the concept.

Left unchecked, Type A behavior can hinder performance because its all-or-none quality can be a strong de-motivator, as you may become hesitant to try new things if you believe that you face "failure" should you not hit your idealized goal. Recently, a nice modification of the Type A concept has taken place in which a more forgiving definition has arisen, this being "adaptive Type A behavior."

This conceptualization says, in essence, that it is fine for you to have high performance expectations, but keep those expectations as goals, and not as absolutes. So, set high goals, work to achieve them, but if you do not reach them, accept that, and do not criticize yourself.

In essence, then, the resulting injunction becomes:

- Aim for an "A" level project, but if you deliver a "B+" level project instead, that is probably acceptable, don't get down on yourself, and celebrate the level that you did achieve

- Learn from the process, set "A" as your next goal, and then see what you can do to hit that goal

The thinking behind crafting high performance goals, but being more accepting of yourself if you do not reach that level, is that you are attempting to keep your motivation high, and your self-concept strong, by not risking it all in all-or-none conceptualizations. In my experience, unchecked maladaptive Type A behavior, due to its inherent "no win" quality for the individual, can create levels of chronic stress that negatively impact the willingness to act.

Let us now look at how stress impacts your performance.

The Impact of Stress on Performance

Stress is a subjectively defined feeling state, based upon many variables, such as your personal style, significant life events during your formative years, your physiological make-up, and your assessment of current events. Thus, your definition of "stress" is ultimately based upon your individual appraisal of a situation, and its possible negative consequences.

Even with such individual factors determining how you define "stress" in life, a broad process definition of stress can still be offered. Kowaslki-Trakofler, Vaught, and Scharf (2012) offer a definition that I find to be very valuable. They cite that stress is:

> …a process by which certain work demands evoke an appraisal process in which perceived demands exceed resources and result in undesirable physiological, emotional, cognitive, and social changes.

If you start to believe that you or a team member may be experiencing performance deficits due to stress, you can apply the following assessment for determining the presence of a "stress induced performance deficit."

This assessment process is something I use to identify performance risks, and after I make my assessment, I can then begin to consider interventions for mediating the impact of the stressor (you can use this assessment process with yourself or for team members).

Below, please find examples of functional areas I look at, with sample problems from each area, and productive actions one can take to reduce the negative performance impacts of stress:

Physiological measures: Team member happens to mention that she is sleeping very poorly.

- Casually ask team member what she has found helpful over the years in improving her sleep pattern

Emotional indicators: Team member appears "down" and is slow to respond when facing cognitive challenges.

- Casually inquire about his current outlook towards the project, his interest level, etc.

Cognitive indicators: Team member is "forgetting" quite a bit, and is late in meeting deadlines.

- Ask her about her current priorities. Look for signs of cognitive overload

Social changes: Team member is withdrawing, thus hindering the degree of knowledge transfer

- *He may be angry*: Offer a neutral comment on your perception that he appears less involved with team members. Look for indicators of unresolved conflict

However, if stress remains at high levels over time, the experience of "chronic stress" may be at hand. Chronic stress (Flannes, 2011, and Flannes, 2013) results in a general decrease in performance and cognitive functioning, as is illustrated in the Yerkes-Dodson Curve. The curve was first described by Yerkes and Dodson (1908), and has extensive implications for many aspects of the human condition. Here is the curve:

Figure 6.3

The Yerkes-Dodson Curve

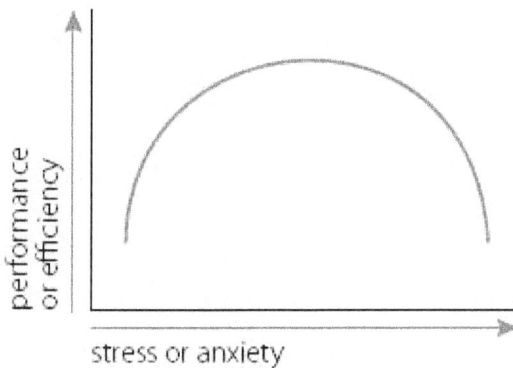

The curve demonstrates that at some point, stress moves from serving as a positive, activating force for increased performance to a negative force. Indeed, in chronic situations, stress evolves into a performance inhibitor. Performance issues (that I have seen) associated with the down slope of the Yerkes-Dodson Curve include the following:

- **Narrowing of attention**: Focusing on just a few variables

- **Overemphasis on short-term decision making**: A desire to "just make it go away"

- **Deterioration of situational awareness**: Blind spots regarding the behavior and intent of others

- **Decision overflow**: Decisions back up, and progress slows

Chronic stress also obviously creates negative affective or emotional states that can hinder performance. Specifically, researchers have noted that emotional states such as anxiety and depression, even when present at subclinical levels, can have deleterious effects on performance, especially in the area of cognitive control, which is a skill needed by the multitasking project professional.

Ng, Chan, and Schlaghecken (2011) have noted that anxiety contributes to a difficulty in controlling emotional responses in tasks involving any component of conflict, plus a tendency to become over-vigilant when some level of cognitive threat is perceived. I believe that when you as project leader are operating under situations that create anxiety:

- You need to be cautious that you do not over-respond (either emotionally, intellectually, or interpersonally), as your ability to inhibit such over-response behaviors will be diminished

- Similarly, you want to remember that during situations involving conflict, you may become disrupted in your ability to control your focus

- Specifically, you may respond in a bifurcated manner—your attention drifting from one topic to another, or your attention becoming hyper-vigilant towards one topic

So, if you assume that research and common sense both suggest that performance will be hindered when you operate under stress, how can you then apply such knowledge to maintain your level of performance? Keep these ideas in mind:

Low level depression (loss of optimism, emotional and intellectual "flatness") can hinder performance:

- Depression creates a cognitive sluggishness which can hinder higher-order intellectual functioning

- If you are feeling "flat" or "low" for an extended period of time, consider that you may be experiencing low level depression, and do what works best for you when you are in that emotional state

When you and/or the team are under stress, focus on developing a flatter communication hierarchy:

- People respond best to crises when there is very open communication among team members

- Communicate, communicate, and then communicate some more!

When the Team Experiences a Crisis or Disaster

The levels of individual and team performance within a project team will suffer when that team experiences a true crisis.

This type of crisis, often described as a critical event (Flannes and Levin, 2005), may have its origin in nature (a natural disaster such as a hurricane or earthquake) or from man-made causes (such as when a team member is injured in an assault).

When these types of crises visit a project team, performance is impacted, especially in those situations where the origins of the crisis are viewed as being man-made. (Additionally, team members who have a history of previous crises or traumas are especially vulnerable to current crises).

For a number of years, writers have described performance deficits that normally arise as the result of individuals or teams going through traumatic events. A basic listing of these performance problems includes:

1. Problems with short term memory, and the learning of new information

2. An increase in interpersonal conflicts, because individuals are more emotionally raw

3. A temporary lack of both productivity and task traction, as the individuals are distracted by natural efforts to process the intense experience

4. A cognitive bias towards the negative, possibly related to the surfacing of old wounds

5. The emergence of apparently irrational responses or unexpected feelings or issues

Here is an example from my personal life of such an unexpected feeling:

> I once lost my house to a huge urban wildfire. For a day or two after the fire, the fire zone was closed to residents, due to safety concerns.
>
> After the neighborhood was finally opened to residents, I and many others walked into the area to see if our homes were still standing.
>
> When I saw that my house was burned to the ground, I immediately felt the natural pain, loss, and confusion inherent in such an experience. However, mixed in with these expected feelings of immense loss were also irrational, or at best, unexpected feelings.
>
> Here is an example of one of these unexpected feelings that I had: "Well, at least *now* I don't have to clean out the garage!"

In sum, be prepared after these events strike you or your team. Stay flexible regarding your immediate expectations of yourself and your team. Many unexpected reactions can surface.

Critical Incident Stress Debriefings

After a team has experienced a traumatic event, some organizations provide the team members with what is described as a critical incident debriefing. These debriefings are structured meetings where an external facilitator walks team members through a discussion of their initial reaction and thoughts about the traumatic event.

The debriefing is not a counseling process, but it can assist individuals in moving forward in processing the event while also keeping their focus on the work at hand.

Critical incident stress debriefings are not suitable for all "cultures" (organizational, national, or ethnic). You as leader should consider whether a debriefing resource is suitable for your culture before a crisis strikes, so that you will have an idea about the level of its acceptance should you consider using one. (Debriefing resources will be known by your human resources department).

For details on the process of a critical incident debriefing, see Flannes and Levin (2005).

Turning Our Attention to Performance Recovery

I have just discussed issues and situations that can negatively impact the performance of both individuals and teams.

Now, the focus for the remainder of the chapter will be the application of "resilience." Resilience is a strategy for recovering from a very difficult situation, returning to desired levels of performance, and then demonstrating the ability to sustain that recovery over time.

(Actually, I should more strongly introduce the resource of resilience. For me, resilience is a very powerful "practice" that leaders should proactively engage in even when not facing a distinct crisis or performance issue. Indeed, I have seen the practice of resilience serve as a stairway, in good times or bad, to reaching the highest levels of performance, where you can operate at your best).

Resilience: Returning to High Levels of Performance —and Beyond

What is resilience? Resilience processes and practices assist you in returning to your pre-crisis level of performance, following your exposure to some sort of upsetting event. Specifically, resilience is often defined as recovery processes involving the following three distinct processes, or stages:

1. You apply your resilience tools, and you are able to recover, returning to the level of performance you had before the crisis

2. Continuing to employ your resilience tools, you are able to sustain the recovery over time

3. Not only can you sustain the recovery, but you are now able to use the lessons learned to transport yourself to even high levels of future performance

I believe that there is no singular definition of resilience that captures its richness. For me, the figure below captures the essence of the resilience process. As you see, Figure 6.4 notes the aspects of recovery, sustainability, and the possibility for future growth.

Figure 6.4

Graphical Representation of the Resilience Process

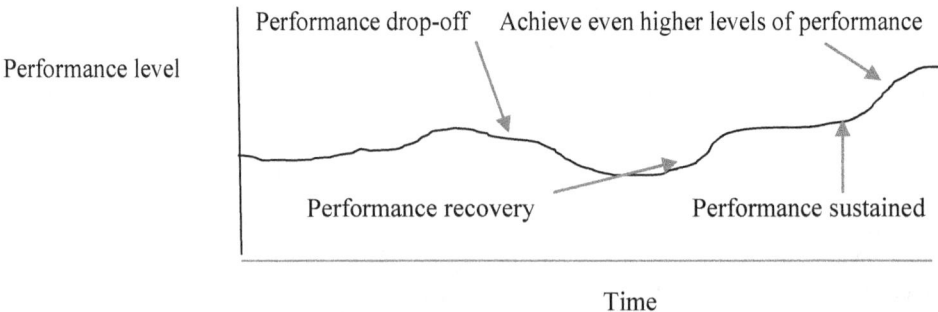

Performance level

Performance drop-off   Achieve even higher levels of performance

Performance recovery   Performance sustained

Time

An Integrative Model

One aspect of resilience that I find very appealing is that resilience is a meld of a number of different approaches to achieving optimal human performance. Resilience incorporates the positive psychology contributions of varied contributors such as Frankl and also Seligman (especially his early work on "learned optimism."). Frankl and Seligman were introduced earlier in this chapter as representatives of the field of positive psychology.

Frankl's core contribution was observational, with his noting which prisoners survived the best while in the concentration camps of World War II. Seligman, on the other hand, has a long history of examining the techniques within the world of positive psychology that help us recovery from difficult situations.

In recent years, Seligman has focused on assisting military personnel in developing resilience tools designed to aid their recovery from battlefield experiences (Cornum, Matthews, and Seligman, 2011). Additionally, Seligman has produced works for the general public, articulating a framework with the goal of helping us "flourish" (Seligman, 2011), even in difficult times.

Smith, Dalen, Wiggins, Tooley, Christopher, and Bernard (2008) have also addressed the benefits of resilience. I see a number of tangible implications for you as leader in their work. Specifically, they found a variety of attitudes or behaviors that were positively correlated with resilience. These variables included:

- The presence in one's life of positive emotions
- Having a purpose in life
- Using active coping strategies

Now, certainly not all of us are born with a psychological constitution which naturally embraces these positive components. However, you can still create and expand such approaches for yourself. The idea here is to insert these practices into your individual make-up, and then you are equipped to demonstrate resilience when needed.

Many Models

As you might expect, there are many models of resilience, but one that I have found to be very helpful is an integrative model from researchers affiliated with Arizona State University (Reich, Zautra, and Hall, 2010). This model of resilience suggests that there are a number of "capacities" that can assist you in recovering from harmful experiences.

Personally, as I have thought about the topic of resilience in recent years, I have settled on the following six variables or attitudes as guideposts for me to use in trying to maintain or expand my resilient abilities.

Search for the Positive Element

In a difficult situation, I believe it is easy to get stuck worrying about the negative, or conversely, taking a too optimistic (naïve?) view implying that "everything will work out just fine." Instead of accepting either of these two extremes, I suggest a more neutral mindset, such as the following:

- "There are many things going wrong here. Let me try to identify two to three things that are going well on this project, and I'll see if I can leverage them towards a positive outcome."

Personally, I find that in difficult situations, I must guard against adopting a negative posture, such as "This project is beyond recovery. There's probably nothing I can do to save it." Again, if I try to create a more neutral mindset (which helps me in my "search for the positive element"), I might try adopting this outlook:

- "This project looks like it is beyond recovery; I'll keep my eyes open during the next few review meetings for ideas we've not thought about before."

Situational Interpersonal Engagement

I believe that you need to have flexibility in order to adapt interpersonally, cognitively (being able to modify your intellectual approach based upon your integrating new information), and emotionally (your ability to realize that your form of successful emotional expression in one cultural setting may not be functional in another culture).

For me, you can achieve a flexible response by doing the following:

- When faced with novel input (either a different culture or a unique type of idea), allow yourself to pause before reacting

- During the pause, notice what you are thinking, as well as what you are feeling, and see if you spot any of your biases or fears of the unknown (or change) starting to surface

- Gather yourself emotionally, "counting to ten" as you work on accepting that this is new territory for you. Take some deep breaths, let yourself relax

- Before putting pressure on yourself to respond appropriately, buy some time by asking open-ended questions. Such questions give you a chance to hear unexpected value from the other person, and an opportunity to calm yourself down physiologically

- And finally, before expecting yourself to offer a cogent response or behavior, use active listening skills to make sure you are understanding what the other person is saying or asking

I have found that gradually allowing myself to work through such a five-point process allows me to remain open to the wisdom found in other settings, or with other people, and therefore stay open to new ways of coping.

Articulate Your Current Personal Mission

Similarly, I believe that to recover from a demanding situation, and become your most resilient, you need to have a purpose for your efforts. Knowing why you need to persevere and remain active is what keeps you going during demanding times.

The *why* becomes the fuel, the passion, and the reason that allows you to remain determined. You cannot remain determined during adversity unless you know why you are asking these demanding efforts of yourself.

Your personal mission can reflect a grand gesture (such as you getting up each morning during a trying period so that you can maintain an income for your family) or it can reflect a less important motive (such as your using your desire to "learn a new skill" as the push that gets you out of bed in the morning).

Regardless of what reason you use to help you get going when you are in a very difficult period, keep its awareness in the forefront of your daily focus.

Strengthen or Expand Your Circle of Engagement

I believe that you do not need a large circle of associates; rather, a smaller circle of friends will nicely suffice. The key to these connections is intimacy, as compared to numbers. You should have people with whom you can be authentic, and a community of involvements that hold meaning for you.

These connections give you a sense of belonging and an engagement that helps propel you forward when you experience dark times. Such connections reduce your experience of isolation, and frequently give you the feeling that "things will probably be OK."

Maintain Your Recovery, Which Also Primes You for Future Growth

Indeed, many people looking at the concept of resilience believe that the sustainability component allows you to grow and perform at even higher levels in the future.

This idea reflects the thinking that the strength and experience that you have gained from the recovery process serves as a platform for the higher levels of performance.

A popular quote which suggests this ability to be even stronger following a crisis is that of the German philosopher Friedrich Nietzsche, who said, "That which does not kill us makes us stronger."

- I think this idea, that we are stronger after surviving a crisis, is very true. I mentioned earlier that I lost my house in a fire. Over time, as we made progress in moving forward, I found that I had changed for the better. I found myself worrying less about issues over which I had no control. Additionally, I was more comfortable in taking life as it presented itself to me, lowering (to some degree) my expectations about how things "should be."

Craft a Myriad of Options for Yourself

Here is a belief that is very simplistic, and is also very powerful:

- When facing any crisis, write down *all* of the options—both serious and outrageous—that you can imagine

This listing (of options that come to mind) will provide you with an increased sense of *personal power* while also adding a dose of humor (as when you list a totally outrageous action that you probably will not take) that can lighten your sense of feeling stuck regarding next steps.

As mentioned, many descriptions of the resilience process exist. I encourage you to integrate the basic concepts of resilience, and then create your own descriptions that describe your specific resilience efforts, using words that have special meaning to you.

In Table 6.5, you will find my own experientially based definitions of resilience.

Table 6.5

Author's Personal Components of Resilience

Component	Description	My Thoughts on How You Can Develop this Component
Search for the positive element	Look for the presence of any realistically positive components in the crisis	Focus on what could go "right" when facing the crisis
Search for situational interpersonal engagement	Your ability to adapt to the different styles of people whom you will encounter	Gradually place yourself in a setting with different types of people; initiate conversations
Articulate your current personal mission to yourself	"I need to pull myself together for the sake of my family"	Ask yourself *why you* are willing to work so hard in order to recover
Strengthen or expand your circle of engagement	Meaningful engagement with individuals and your community	Spend time with a few close friends and a few meaningful community members
Craft a myriad of options	Create a long list of coping approaches and experiences, covering all aspects of being human	Keeps your emotional and cognitive focus in the present, focusing on what you can do *now* to improve things

I feel more equipped in my life by having my own resilience plan. I can look forward with a greater comfort about the unknown, empowered by the knowledge that I "have a plan" when bad times hit.

Stress Management vs. Resilience: Comparisons

Both "stress management" and "resilience" are often discussed when considering performance enhancement and performance recovery efforts following difficult events.

Before concluding the chapter, I want to summarize their differences, and offer my thoughts on why I think **resilience** offers more potency and applicability for project management leaders than does just **stress management**. These thoughts are presented in Table 6.6.

Table 6.6

Comparative Differences Between Stress Management and Resilience

Core Variables	Stress Management	Application of Resilience
Temporal perspective	Intervention is often applied after the fact	Resilience practices are geared towards a here-and-now application
Intervention goal	Symptom reduction	More powerful goals, such as returning to previous high level of performance
Location where "practiced"	Often away from work setting: off-site (such as gym or the park)	On-site and off-site, due to its integrative approach
Overall goal	Symptom reduction and a positive subjective feeling	Symptom reduction, plus enhancement and increase of performance (plus an ancillary increase of the "quality of life" experience)

Clearly, both stress management and resilience are valid approaches for moderating stress or other reactions from crisis events. Personally, I just find the resilience model to be more robust and easier to access conceptually.

Resilience: A Future Focus

Resilience, I believe, will garner more and more attention in upcoming years. Its origin is in the world of helping people recover from traumatic events, but its proactive nature will assure it a spot in the general literature of performance enhancement.

Project leaders have described resilience to me as being a tangible, process- oriented approach that can be easily inserted into a project leader's tool box. Keep your eyes on the field of resilience, as it will be appearing, I believe, in more and more discussions of performance enhancement.

Chapter 7
Creating an Effective and Task-Driven Team Culture

Steven Flannes

Effective team cultures don't just happen. They are not the result of good luck, nor are they guaranteed just because your team is composed of very bright and motivated professionals.

As with much of this book, I am not in this chapter attempting to provide a broad overview on the traditional key processes involved in effective team building. I will leave that to others, such as Yeager and Nafukho (2012).

Instead, I present specific approaches, techniques, and personal lessons I have gathered from my career as a leader and a psychologist. I believe these approaches are not often considered when one looks at creating an effective team culture, but I have found them to be very helpful in a variety of settings.

Quality team cultures are created and nurtured by leaders displaying an artful hand in synthesizing and leading a disparate group of people, each with conflicting loyalties. Creating an effective, goal directed team culture would certainly be easier if you were able to hand-pick your team members, based on your hope of getting "the right people." Unfortunately, as you know, you rarely have the luxury of hand-picking your team roster. You often must take who you are given, and make the best of it. That is not easy, but that's the world of project leadership.

This dilemma of not being able to choose your team members is diplomatically addressed on page 225 of PMI'S PMBOK (2008), where leaders are instructed that they will "*acquire* the project team" members. The key word here is "acquire," which calls to mind the idea that we *acquire* our family members, but we get to choose our friends. Such is life in project leadership, due to variables such as outsourcing and subcontractors, as well as labor agreements, politics, and who knows what else.

But, enough of my complaining about not getting to choose my team! Let's now look at what you do to create a high functioning team with a special culture, even when you do not get to choose the members.

What Does PMBOK Say?

PMI's PMBOK (Project Management Institute, 2008) offers a clear and firm direction regarding the fundamentals for delivering successful projects. The PMBOK guidelines serve as a strong foundation for project leaders to use in creating an efficient team culture, and include goals such as having knowledge of organizational influences, best approaches for managing human resources, and using charters to create clear expectations. Clearly, the various competencies and skills presented in PMBOK provide you with a good start towards creating effective teams.

However, I now want to look at what I think are more subtle and powerful variables that will help you create a task-driven culture. I believe that the subtle variables presented in this chapter can help create a cohesive and effective team culture in our world of unpredictability, ambiguity, and the rapid deployment of new technologies.

As with all the other skills in this book, these skills require you to make a personal commitment to your own ongoing personal skills development.

The first variable that I want to consider towards creating a high performance team culture is to look once again, but from a different perspective, at the core leadership behavior that melds individuals together into cohesive teams.

Leader's Interpersonal Behavior

I think it is important to briefly review key leadership attributes that were presented earlier in the book. These are qualities and behaviors I believe all leaders must have.

First, the leader must have effective interpersonal communication skills, and for this topic I refer you back to Chapter 5. In that chapter, I stated that four communication skills are crucial for leaders (also, see Flannes and Levin, 2005). These four skills involve:

1. Your ability to *ask open-ended questions*, which give you the opportunity to hear a variety of statements from the stakeholder

2. The ability to *use active listening* to make sure you are accurately hearing (encoding) what the stakeholder is saying

3. Your skill at *tracking the communication*, which involves both your ability to perceive when the discussion is heading off track, and your assertiveness in offering comments that will bring the discussion back on track

4. Your comfort in *using reframing comments* which can help a team member with a negative or defeatist attitude begin to see that the glass might be half full after all

The second category of leadership interpersonal competencies required for developing an effective team culture is the leader's level of emotional intelligence (EQ). As I mentioned in Chapter 5, EQ involves your ability to have self-awareness, your skill in moderating your expression of emotions, plus your competency in perceiving the uniqueness and style of the individuals who constitute your team.

Two other leadership attributes are also crucial for you to have in order to create the effective team culture. One of these qualities is the ability to demonstrate congruence between what you say you will do and the behavior you actually display. Said differently, you want to be sure your actions match your statements. And finally, the last core leadership ability that you must have for creating an effective team culture is your ability to proactively manage the inevitable conflict that will exist on your team.

Therefore, to be a leader who can create an effective team culture:

1. You must be skilled in interpersonal communication

2. You need to have mastery of your emotions, plus an understanding of the emotions of others

3. You have to follow through on what you say you will do

4. You must develop a decent level of comfort and skill in managing the conflicts of team life

Missing any of these four foundational leadership qualities, you will be hampered in creating the effective team culture that you desire. An overview of these interpersonal leadership skills, with examples, is presented in Table 7.1.

Table 7.1

Leader Interpersonal Skills Required for Creating Effective Team Cultures

Skill	Example	Benefits of Skill	Problems when Skill Is Absent
Asking *open-ended questions*	"Please tell me about what's working and what's not working on the estimate."	Assists leader in gathering more information. Creates positive tone with team member	Leader misses key information, and comes across as not interested in team member
Using *active listening*	"Sounds like you want me to help with the testing and quality issues?"	Makes certain that both parties are in agreement as to the points being discussed and the action being planned	Leader and team member may be heading in different directions, not realizing that such a disparity exists
Tracking discussion, content or purpose	"I think we are talking about a second topic now. Let's go back and cover your concerns about the testing."	Helps keep the discussion moving forward in a linear manner, increasing the effectiveness of the interaction	The discussion wanders from point to point, increasing frustration and a lack of efficiency (especially during group discussions)
Ability to *reframe* a negative situation	"Yes, I realize you are stuck. But, what might be a way you can turn this impasse into an advantage?"	Assists the team member in accessing their creativity, while also reducing the stress of the leader	Negativity that is not reframed pollutes the atmosphere of the team
EQ	Ability to perceive the emotional needs of others, and to manage one's own emotions	Emotions are moderated and are not a disruptive force within the team	Too much emphasis is placed on the intellect, and not enough on the interpersonal factors of team dynamics
Congruence of words and action	Following through in tangible ways on commitments that have been made verbally or in writing	Engenders trust from team members while reducing ambiguity	Lack of congruence creates a cynical tone within team, and a decrease in motivation
Willingness and ability to actively address conflict	"Before we go farther, I think we need to acknowledge that we have some strong disagreements."	Creates greater efficiency within team while also reducing the build-up of resentments	Unaddressed conflict derails team progress, reduces informal knowledge sharing, and is a prime contributor to creating a poorly motivated team

Having reviewed these interpersonal skills, let us now shift our focus to looking at an interesting assortment of variables, team tones and attitudes, and structures and processes that you can put in place to create a positive team culture.

Developing Team Trust

Trust is a desired state of affairs in all interpersonal relationships. For the purposes of this chapter, I am viewing trust as a subjectively held belief (usually involving positive attributions held by one entity towards another) that exits in varying degrees between team members and leader, as well as among team members.

Trust can be defined as one might define good art: you know it when you experience it. I think of trust as referring to:

- Your belief that the other person keeps your best interests in mind

- Your sense that the team member will do what she promised to do

- Your assessment that while a specific team member may be a nasty, critical person, you can at least "trust" that this person will continue to behave this way in meetings, allowing you to plan accordingly. (So, in this example, "trust" might be defined as your believing that the team member will display consistent, even if negative, behavior over time).

As leader, you really can't get away with offering generalizations (in this case, about trust) during the formation of your team culture. Rather than saying something general like "I believe it is important for all of us to create a culture in which we can trust each other," you should offer specific examples of trust-creating behaviors as a way of generating group discussion about a definition of trust.

For example, one project leader may define trust as:

- Following through on a commitment that I make to a team member

- Not talking negatively behind a team member's back

- Actively speaking up when I have a conflict with a team member

- Always trying to do what is best for the team and the project

Such self-disclosure opens up discussion on how the other members of this team define trust. In this conversation, you then have a chance to look for both commonalities and variances, whether due to differences in personal style or in cultural background.

Personally, I define trust as involving two core components:

1. The degree of consistency about which a team member completes his or her task in a timely manner, adhering to the established quality guidelines and within the budget allocated for that task (in essence, a good faith embrace of the triple constraint).

2.   The degree to which one displays character traits of a selfless placing of "team first," as well as a well-intentioned approach to all team interpersonal interactions

Research has recently focused heavily on the importance of trust in creating a productive environment within teams. Rusman, Van Bruggen, Sloep, Icke, and Koper (2012) state that an important variable in developing trust within a virtual team is making a positive first impression. Presenting an impression of trustworthiness during these first interactions is viewed by these authors as a requirement for effective collaboration.

Dorairaj, Noble, and Malik (2012) looked at the importance of trust in virtual teams that were operating within an Agile framework. They found that there were a number techniques that were helpful in developing trust. Some of these techniques included the creation of a team identity, frequent in-person interaction between team members, as well as formal and informal vehicles for knowledge sharing.

Conscientiousness as a Trust Fundamental

Before leaving this discussion on trust, I want to mention a related concept for you to keep in mind as you create the atmosphere for an effective team culture. O'Neil and Allen (2011) found that the personality attribute of "conscientiousness" is the best predictor for high levels of team performance. The importance of conscientiousness appears in much of the research on the topics of leadership and effective team behavior.

As a leader wanting to create a culture noted for team member conscientiousness, you can:

- Define "conscientious," as you see it, with your team

- Implement a team-involved discussion of various definitions of conscientiousness

- Role model conscientious behavior in all of your interactions with team members and other stakeholders

What Motivates? To Each His Own

Because you are a leader, you are naturally concerned with how to be a motivating influence for your team members.

But, what is motivation? How can you define it? Clearly, the concept of motivation has been explored over the years by looking at Theory X (people need constant attention and supervision in order to perform), Theory Y (people are naturally looking for ways to contribute), and a variety of other theoretical formulations (See Peterson, 2007, for a good overview on theories of motivation).

Apply Individual Differences

I believe, however, that the best way to visualize the concept of motivation is to stay away from a tight adherence to a certain theory. Instead, I believe that the most effective way to view motivation is through the window of individual differences. Your job as the leader, therefore, becomes one of knowing the wishes, styles, and quirks of your individual team members, so that you can apply this knowledge of their individual differences to the goal of motivating.

I can best describe the importance of individual differences by relating a story that I have heard somewhere along the way in my career. The story illustrates the idea that different people may perform the same work, but for different reasons. Not a brilliant or new idea, but one worth remembering. Here is the story:

> Somewhere in Europe in the 17th century, a traveler on foot approached a small village, where he came across six stone masons who were working on a structure that would become the region's main house of worship.
>
> As he paused to rest, the traveler asked each of the stone masons *why* he was working on this building, given the work appeared grueling, and the temperature was extreme. Here is what each of the stone masons said:
>
> *First stone mason*: "I took this job so that a young lady in a neighboring village would find me worthy and responsible, and would marry me."
>
> *Second stone mason*: "I am only working here because my father is ill, and I need to support all of my family."
>
> *Third stone mason*: "This is my craft, and I am working here to learn new skills that will serve me well."
>
> *Fourth stone mason*: "My labor is offered here in service of building a meeting place where my community will gather for weddings and celebrations."
>
> *Fifth stone mason*: "While this work is hard, it is so much better than the work I did in the mines."
>
> *Sixth stone mason*: "This work is a spiritual offering from me, as it honors my faith."

Same profession. Same project. Different reasons, or motivations, for doing the work. Such is the concept of individual differences as a source of motivation.

These ideas and examples on the importance of considering the unique sources of motivation for a number of different individuals is continued in the next section, where I offer thoughts on how to consider personality as a source for motivation.

Develop a Motivating Environment by Working with Team Member Personality

Over my career, I have come to believe that your goal as the leader should be to lead efforts towards *creating a motivating environment* within your team, as compared to a focus on *how to motivate a team member*.

A focus on how to motivate a team member runs the risk of your viewing the motivation process in a mechanistic way, almost like motivation becomes *something you do to the team member*, just as a physical therapist may work on a team member's bad knee. Conversely, a focus on creating a motivating environment is more effective, because it acknowledges the dynamic nature of individual motivation and it carries the implication that the team member himself needs to be involved in articulating and defining his own sources of motivation.

(For additional comments on the concept of creating a motivating team environment, see Peterson, 2007).

A component of creating a motivating environment is your ability to look at team members as individuals, each with a unique motivation make-up. The application of individual differences, which has been discussed elsewhere in this book, is a very helpful tool to use in nurturing a motivating team environment. There are many individual differences models that you can use, and we can again refer to the Myers-Briggs model.

Leverage the Team's Individual Differences

The Myers-Briggs Type Indicator (MBTI) can be used to describe different sources of motivation for the various personality styles. The project leader with either formal or informal knowledge of team members' MBTI styles can use this knowledge to effectively motivate individuals.

Below are some ideas about how you can use the MBTI concepts in creating a motivating environment, energizing the various members of your team. These thoughts are based upon a presentation that I made in 1998 to a gathering of project professionals (Flannes, 1998).

- **Extrovert (outgoing, seeks interaction)**: Have this person focus on the relationship aspects of the project, such as interactions with stakeholders

- **Introvert (quiet, reflective, inner-directed):** Offer this person work that requires extended periods of concentration, possibly working alone

- **Sensing (pragmatic, practical, here-and-now focus):** Give this person work that has a distinct completion point and can be measured in concrete terms

- **Intuitive (conceptual, big-picture orientation):** Put this person to work on the strategic and design portions of the project, relating the project's objectives to the program's strategic objectives

- **Thinking (logical, analytical decision making):** Present this individual with tasks requiring quantitative skills or analysis

- **Feeling (people-focused, subjective orientation for decision making):** Allow this person to be in roles involving nurturing and customer relationship management

- **Judging (orderly, structured, closure oriented):** Permit this person the chance to create schedules, budgets, and project closure systems

- **Perceiving (flexible, spontaneous, prefers to leave options open)**: Direct this person towards situations requiring trouble-shooting

Ask Them: The Best Approach

Related to using this knowledge of a team member's personal style towards the goal of creating a motivating environment is the idea of also using your awareness of team members' career anchors (see Chapter 2 for a description of career anchors) for motivation.

However, when using a personal style system such as the MBTI or the career anchors, it is important, as I have said earlier in the book, to not to take the system too literally. Systems such as the MBTI are excellent for giving you a window to look through when thinking about motivation. However, the best way to create a motivating setting for someone is to ask them what motivates them—and to listen carefully to what they tell you. Asking them what is motivating is such a simple idea, but I find that it is something that many of us do not do when we are in leadership roles.

Melding Individuals into Teams

The previous section on individual differences looked at the team from the micro level. In this section, I describe how you can meld these individuals into a team. I will not address traditional topics such as team building, as they are nicely covered elsewhere. Rather, I will focus on some interesting and unusual perspectives on how to create a team from a set of individuals.

One such interesting approach is that of looking to create "personality balance" on your team. Yeh, Wei, Wei, and Lei (2012) present the belief that when a team is balanced along certain key team roles, the team will perform better than when such balance does not exist. In their investigation, Yei et.al. describe the optimal team personality as one that contains a number of different role functions, including the *coordinator,* the *shaper*, and the *specialist.*

Other researchers have examined the nature of interpersonal relationships within teams operating on transnational levels, highlighting the importance of such relationships in creating an effective team culture. Zimmerman (2010) brings up an excellent point when she encourages you to look beyond outdated conceptualizations of how teams function. She notes that the bulk of previous research has endorsed a linear model of team functioning, believing that team dynamics can be explained through the "input-process-output" model. Zimmerman offers what she terms a "configural" perspective on team functioning.

Her configural perspective suggests that social systems (such as teams) are complex, involving a multitude of moving parts that influence each variable in reciprocal manners, thus making cause and effect determinations of social interactions impossible to identify. Additionally, she notes that team interactions, especially in transnational settings, do not unfold in a linear manner in which you as the leader can easily identify cause and effect relationships.

Transnational teams would appear to be more three dimensional in nature (my phrasing), in which variables (people) interact in unpredictable manners to influence team tone and structure.

Mixing Different Generations into One Team

The workforce of the future will continue to be represented by a variety of different generations, due in part to the fact that fewer and fewer members of the older generations are completely retiring from the workplace. People are working longer, and are able to do so because of vehicles such as part-time positions or contract opportunities. Such generation variety creates another "melding" challenge for you.

Research efforts are now focusing on this challenge of melding individuals from different generations into a team. For example, Anantatmula and Shrivasta (2012) speak of the importance of melding Generation Y individuals (those team members born between 1980 and 2001) into the workforce in general, and into teams in particular.

In presenting their research on the Generation Y age cohort, Anantatmula and Shrivasta offer some important suggestions for you to remember when melding different generation team members into a highly functioning team. These suggestions on how to integrate the best contributions from different generations are below:

Generation (Years of Birth)	What Motivates This Generation?
Silent: 1922 to 1945	Desires to demonstrate perseverance and loyalty
Baby Boomers: 1946 to 1964	Wants to demonstrate ability and the value of their contributions
Generation X: 1965 to 1979	Prefers to work in non-hierarchical structures and achieve work-life balance
Generation Y: 1980 to 2001	Desires advancement and rewards with less need for social approval

While it can be dangerous to take comments on the characteristics of different generations too literally, such a focus can still be worthwhile, if used judiciously. Use these age group generalizations as starting points for identifying the nature of the people whom you are leading.

Now, I want to approach the topic of creating an effective team culture by talking about what *not to do*.

Minimize Your Mistakes in Motivating

As the leader, you should experiment with different approaches to creating a motivating environment, but you should also be aware of motivational efforts that do not work well.

In my experience, I have found that as a leader, it is quite easy to fall into the pattern of offering clichés, generalizations, and stereotypes when wanting to motivate. These risks are especially prominent when the leader is over-worked or fatigued. Here are five well-intentioned, but nevertheless cliché-based motivation strategies and beliefs that I have either encountered, or have used myself:

"Whatever motivates me will motivate others."

This belief is an extension of the assumption that others want to be treated the same way you want to be treated. People are often motivated by the same approaches, but not always. Do not make assumptions about what will motivate someone—ask them!

"The best project leader is a strong cheerleader."

Cheerleading can be an important part of managing people, but the project leader needs to be careful not to overdo it. Cheerleading can certainly be a positive effort, but it needs to be used carefully. Often, the best way to motivate people is to let them come up with the inspiration and energy for their own actions, free from outside cheerleading.

"These people are professionals. They don't need motivating!"

Project professionals are generally self-motivating, following an inner drive that leads to achievement and productivity. However, nearly everyone profits from outside sources of motivation, particularly on projects that are lengthy or frustrating.

"I'll motivate them when there is a problem."

This approach to motivation takes the old adage that says "No news is good news" to an extreme. Unfortunately, people tend not to tell you when their motivation is starting to suffer. Rather, the level of motivation usually needs to get seriously low before most people speak up and address the issue. The skilled motivator takes a proactive approach to motivating the team, not waiting for motivation issues to surface.

"I'll treat everyone the same. People like that, and it will be motivating for them."

It is safe to assume that it is important to treat everyone the same on issues of basic fairness and job performance standards. But, it is also important to recognize team members as individuals, especially when creating strategies to motivate each of the individuals on the team. Different things motivate people at different points in their lives.

Clearly, these motivation mistakes can be a hindrance when you are working to create an effective team culture. However, the presence on your team of "free- riders" can be an even stronger negative force that can complicate your work in creating the desired team culture.

What to Do About "Free Riders"

Another approach to addressing personality variables that can impact team culture and performance, but in a negative way, is described by He (2012). *He* speaks about the negative impact that team member "free-riding" can have on team performance.

Free riding (I personally enjoy a synonym term that *He* also presents: "social loafing") is that behavior within a group where a team member does not contribute his or her share of work effort, but because it's a team environment, receives a disproportionate amount of reward, when considering the ratio between effort expended and reward obtained.

As you know from your experience, such free riders can sabotage a team climate very quickly, creating resentment, diminished information transfer, and reduced creativity. (The only other negative team force that I have seen that comes close to equaling the negative impact of free riding would be that of unaddressed conflict).

So, what can you do if you are leading a team, and you have a free riding team member? *He* suggests two interventions: designing the reward system to encourage social cooperation, and designing negative sanctions for those who free ride. I would say that these sound like wise interventions, but they are often not appropriate when you are leading a matrix, projectized team, and therefore do not have the authority to construct such reward systems.

Then, what are your options? *He* suggests the idea of introducing efforts that increase team morale, and the idea of reducing the size of the team (reducing the ability to "hide," in my view). I also believe that you can be effective with free riders by your being assertive and direct. Speak quickly to free-riding behavior as soon as you see it, because such behavior does not usually change on its own.

Structural Considerations for Creating Effective Team Cultures

Your goal of developing an effective team culture can also be considered from the perspective of looking at what you can adopt within your team that increase the chances for your team having an effective culture. The next section of this chapter will explore some of these structural initiatives that are at your disposal.

Formal Communication vs. Informal Cross-Functional Communication

One such structural initiative, this one being in the form of team communication vehicles, is presented by Boerner, Shaffner, and Gebert (2012). These authors explored the issues presented when new services development (NSD) groups are tasked with creating innovative services.

Boerner et al. state that such NSD teams are popular in service sectors such as consulting and banking, where organizations are continually needing to innovate their services in order to articulate their added value in sectors with extreme competition. Their results suggested that informal cross-functional communication is more effective in enhancing *knowledge generation* while formal team meeting communication was more effective in *knowledge integration.*

You have probably witnessed these behaviors in your own work.

For example, think about the creativity that you have seen emerge when people with unique perspectives gather and communicate, with no agenda or task goal. Likewise, you have probably also experienced how few things really get done when such a lack of structure continues into meetings where things need to be accomplished.

Within your team, you will want to develop a culture where you encourage off-line informal discussions between cross-functional professionals. Additionally, you will also need to create a team culture with the needed "infrastructure" to absorb generated knowledge into a project specification rubric. These are two very difficult things to do, and it takes a leader with sophistication to be able to know when to move the group from one way of thinking to the other.

Obviously, there are no constant guidelines about when and how to do this. Rather, you must assess the needs of the moment, and then move the focus back and forth, just as an orchestra conductor might guide her musicians from one emphasis to another.

What "Form" of Project Management is Right for Your Team?

When working to establish your team's culture, you should also be paying attention to the size of your company. Specifically, the work of Turner, Ledwith, and Kelly (2010) suggests that the size of the company impacts how formally or informally the project management tenets should be exercised within the team in question.

Turner et al. found that smaller sized companies needed to have team cultures where the project management methodology is exerted in more informal ways. They also presented ideas related to what team culture is preferred by different countries, noting that Ireland and Sweden preferred more informal team cultures, while teams in Austria desired more formal, directive team cultures.

These results remind me of the requirement for you to be flexible in your cognitive approach for establishing the infrastructure for your team, crafting approaches that are tailored to the specific components of your team. Once again, as I have done in earlier sections of the book, I find myself encouraging you to identify "individual differences," in this case differences in company size, or differences in company nationality.

Importance of Cultural Boundary Spanners

An additional "structural" initiative you can undertake in creating effective team cultures is the idea of looking for "cultural boundary spanners."

This informal team function is held by a team member, especially in cross-cultural teams, who can "influence performance by spanning cultural and linguistic boundaries..." (Di Marco and Taylor, 2009). When cultural boundary spanners (CBSs) can be identified within project networks, these authors have noted an increase of initial communication within global project teams, as compared to project teams that do not have a CBS. Additionally, teams with a CBS, when compared to cross-cultural teams without a CBS, completed tasks quicker.

But, who are these cultural boundary spanners, and where can you find them? The answers to these questions are both simple and complex.

The simple answer: CBSs are team members (not necessarily formal leaders) whose background, life experiences, and cross-cultural skill set allow this person to serve as a cultural translator, using their knowledge of culture and language to unite team members, increasing the level of project collaboration.

For me, synonyms for CBSs include: liaison, translator, facilitator, and guide. Additionally, the CBS is described as a bridge maker and a blender by other writers (Butler, Zander, Mockaitis, and Sutton, 2012).

I also believe that cultural boundary spanners are often people who:

1. Have no formal leadership imperative, but always seem ready to help

2. Are cross-culturally literate, appear to move with great comfort between groups

3. Have qualities such as humility, trustworthiness, and a personal presence that encourages people to seek them out

4. Are receptive towards others, and appear "available" when one approaches them

5. See differences in people as a variable to leverage, and not just "manage"

The complex answer is that such individuals are not labeled, or known as a CBS, within their respective organizations. Additionally, senior executives who do not hold a deep appreciation for the benefits of such cultural translators may give little credence to the importance of their involvement. Often, such executives fall victim to a mindset that says, "We already have procedures and systems in place that bring people together; let's not over-think this issue."

So, as leader, you may not be able to force the insertion into your team of an identified CBS. But, what you can do is the following:

- Look for such people on your team who come the closest to matching the descriptions of a CBS

- Reach out to that person, encouraging their buy-in to the concept of their serving in this informal, but important role

- Let other team members know that you have asked this individual to serve in the role of a CBS, and encourage team members to reach out to this person for cultural guidance

- Should you have no one on your team who even approximates the definition of a CBS, talk with your team about the benefits of CBS skills, and encourage the team to look for ways to create a CBS mentality within the team, with a reminder as to the collaboration benefits and performance benefits of such a presence

I believe that the cultural boundary spanner, ultimately, plays the sophisticated role of integrator, creating safe avenues for interpersonal navigation and for informal knowledge sharing.

Creating Effective Team Cultures: Emerging Tools

New approaches and new trends are emerging that address the subject of what attitudes, processes, or technologies aid in the development of an effective team culture. This section will very briefly identify two of these new approaches and trends, which include the application of social media, and the futurist contributions of brain-based measures for determining team composition.

Social Media in PM Communications

The strong influence of social media has spread into the world of project management. Remidez and Jones (2012) address the use of social media in project management communication, noting that such media can help engender trust within team members who are geographically and temporally dispersed.

They point out that traditional email has become inadequate to address the sophisticated levels of communication required in project management, and that software vendors have responded to this need by developing a variety of social media-based offerings, including Twitter-like progress updates, and project news delivered in a Facebook-like manner.

One can only speculate on the rapid growth rate within projectized work that social media will experience in the upcoming years. It will be interesting to see how project professionals who have not grown up with the Twitter and Facebook mindset will adjust to such changes. And just think about your challenges as the leader, should you have a multi-generational team (quite likely, due to the previously stated fact that professionals are working longer than before) in which not all team members are comfortable, not to mention competent, in the evolving world of social media.

Clearly, the role of social media in aiding communication and building trust (thus assisting in the development of effective team cultures), is just beginning. Many exciting and unseen benefits will emerge over time. Such trust building benefits will be especially helpful in cross-national or virtual teams.

Assembling Teams Based Upon Brain-Based Measures

The field of cognitive neuroscience maps the relationships between brain functioning and individual behavior and attitudes. Woolley et. al (2007) note that neural imaging studies have demonstrated that individual differences in brain activity can be applied to predicting team performance on certain tasks.

In their work, they found that small teams whose members were given role assignments that were congruent with their individual abilities (defined via the various brain-based measures) performed better that small teams where such congruence was not established.

Certainly, the interest and the resources are not in place for project management to be using these brain-based methods for assembling teams, but it definitely is an interesting idea. My guess is that brain-based methods will first be employed in academic and educational settings, where project management students will have the opportunity to receive brain-based information as to their ideal competencies, and they will then use this knowledge in targeting and self-selecting organizations and job function niches that are compatible with this knowledge that they acquired earlier.

Create a Peer Coaching Atmosphere

There are so many forces out there (this book included) that trumpet the idea that project success is highly dependent upon the leadership and interpersonal skills of the leader.

Indeed, at my seminars, project leaders often appear to be carrying the burden of believing that project success is primarily dependent on their skills as leader. This heavy emphasis on leadership exists throughout our culture. Notice how many high profile and successful leaders have become cultural celebrities and icons, with their every move or decision dissected for lessons learned.

However, Hackman and Wageman (2007) caution us about putting too much of the burden for project success on the backs of leaders. They term this tendency the leadership attribution error and define it as the "tendency to identify the leader as the main cause of collective performance." Their work suggests that you should definitely focus on your behavior and leadership skills, but you should also not lose track of other variables that impact the culture and performance of your team, taking some of that burden away from you, the project leader.

One approach that helps me keep this perspective in mind when I am in leadership roles is my effort to create a team culture noted for a high level of "peer coaching." A team with a high level of peer coaching is known for having members who informally serve as mentors, partners, and problem solvers for other team members.

In a team noted for peer coaching, members are freely interacting with each other, seeking guidance from peers, while also offering assistance to the same peers. The project leader remains central to the team function, and certainly steps in when needed to address a problem, but those interactions are more the exception than the norm.

In such a team culture, the leader balances the responsibility of being a problem solver with the need to create engagement among members, so that team members reach out to other team members when a problem surfaces, and not just to the project leader.

In essence, the leader is saying to the team member seeking assistance "Yes, I can help with that problem, but I think that Frank knows more about this than I do. I'd suggest you reach out to him." Such referring out to others creates an atmosphere of first level problem solving, greater knowledge sharing, and a set of team members who are more able to expand their individual levels of expertise by being of service to others.

In closing, look to find that balance point between being an active problem solver and creating the peer coaching process among your team members. Such peer coaching creates an environment that is good for you personally (less leader work and personal stress) and also for the team (more first level problem solving, achieved at a quicker pace).

Common Sense: Team Culture Basics

As with almost all group experiences in life, project team members take their cues from the leader when establishing behavior norms and expectations for the group.

If you are the leader, you are the key force for establishing an effective and goal directed team culture. You set the norm here, and therefore remember that team members will place more emphasis on *what you do* and *how you are* than they will on *what you say*.

Lead by example, be present and congruent, and speak directly to the behaviors and attitudes that you want for your team.

Once again, effective cultures do not happen just because you have bright, good people. If you are the leader, then you must take the first steps in creating the culture you desire, and then you must nourish that culture over the life of the project.

Chapter 8
Managing Conflict:
Innovative Approaches That Work

Steven Flannes

There are three fundamental beliefs that I find important for addressing conflict situations within your team, or with outside stakeholders. These beliefs include:

- You should aim to *manage* conflicts, as compared to attempting to *resolve* them

- In addressing conflicts, focus on what you *need,* as compared to what you *want*

- Focus on managing the conflict *relationship*, and not the *person*

You as leader must find ways to be comfortable and skillful in managing conflict. If you do not hold such confidence or skill, you may face consequences such as:

- Work flow blockage

- Possible project shutdown due to interpersonal issues

- Lack of informal knowledge transfer

- Negative team member emotions (such as anger, resentment, "compliance behavior," or apathy)

Conversely, if you do have effective conflict management skills, you can contribute to a number of positive outcomes for your team, and also for your project. A sample of these benefits is presented below:

- Increased leadership effectiveness due to accelerated project progression

- Strong interpersonal connections. These bonds are the interpersonal "currency" needed to make things happen

- Increase of team "trust"

- Greater chances for project creativity. Conflict that is "managed" can be a source of energy and positive friction that leads to new directions

- Lingering issues addressed, and therefore greater personal piece of mind

- Enhanced reputation, leading to an increase in career options

Managing, Not Resolving

Previously, when I have written or spoken about the subject of project conflict, I have referred to the topic as "conflict resolution." Implied in my choosing that term was my apparent belief that conflicts could be "resolved"—finished, completed, put to rest. Some conflicts can be "resolved" in a neat and tidy manner, but most cannot.

(It is my experience that the conflicts that can be "resolved" in such a tidy manner are conflicts that are based in a *lack of information*. For example, I might have such a conflict with you if I thought we would have four engineers for the project, and you believed we would have only two engineers. So, when the "facts" are clarified, and we both have the same information, we can get our numbers straight, and are then able to neatly end our conflict).

These days, however, I believe it is more realistic to focus on "managing" conflicts as compared to trying to "resolve" them. Why this change of terminology? I think "manage" is a more accurate term because dynamics within projectized teams have become increasingly more complex and fluid, hence my current belief that trying to "resolve" a conflict would be like trying to hit a moving target. Managing a conflict, thus, becomes both more realistic and practical.

Focus on What You *Need*, Not Just on What You *Want*

During a conflict, it is important to focus on what you *need* for conflict management, as compared to what you *want*. Too often, we focus on what we *want* in addressing a conflict (I want to get all of my requests, I want to be seen as right, I want to fix this conflict once and for all, etc.).

The alternative goal—of focusing on what you *need*—allows you to let go of the hope of having a perfect ending to the conflict. Such a complete fix is unrealistic, given the expected contradictory goals among vast numbers of stakeholders, changes in scope and resource allocation, plus the lack of control to get what you want when working within projectized environments.

Manage the *Relationship*, Not the *Person*

One simple but important goal should remain at the forefront in your thinking as you address a conflict with another individual: Your task is to focus on changing what happens *between* you and the stakeholder with whom you have the conflict.

If you focus on modifying what happens *between* you and the other party, you will likely feel less personally vulnerable and will also be able to conceptualize a broader array of possible responses.

As you focus on the relationship, remember to be aware of two traps that leaders often do not see. These traps are:

- Debating the other person
  - You as leader wanting to be seen as "right"

These two traps are discussed below.

Stay Away from Debating

Many exchanges during conflicts involve the parties debating each other about the wisdom of their arguments. However, debating another stakeholder can be like pouring gasoline on a fire. A bad situation only gets worse.

Should you find yourself debating a team member or stakeholder, the best things to do are:

- Stop offering any counterpoint, and shift into a listening mode, hoping that the listening mode alters the direction of the discussion

- If the listening mode does not reduce the debating behavior of the other person, then you may need to set limits on the time for the discussion, take a break, or reschedule the discussion for a later time

Let Go of Wanting to Be "Right"

Bright and verbally articulate individuals can easily fall into the trap during a conflict of wanting to be seen as "right." The desire to be seen as right can increase when you are in the leadership role: aren't leaders supposed to know what's going on?

As a leader, rather than focus during a conflict on being perceived as right, it is more effective to focus on being perceived as "competent." By demonstrating competence during a conflict, you are investing in problem solving, as compared to position defending.

How Do You Know You Are in a Conflict?

Before I present thoughts about specific techniques for managing conflict, I want to first address a more basic consideration: how do you actually know when you are in a conflict?

Obviously, many conflicts are obvious, as the cues are just so transparent. However, there are many situations in projectized work environments when you may have difficulty in determining that you are actually involved in a conflict. Here are three such situations.

Personality Attribute-Based Conflicts

In many ways, this is the toughest type of conflict to address, because the other party, in essence, is angry with you just because they do not like you (which could be because they have issues with your sex, age, race, personality, appearance, etc.). You may be dealing with this type of conflict when you notice:

- A free-floating sense of disapproval or verbal aggression coming from the other person

- Nothing you do seems to improve their treatment of you

- Everything else considered, you come away saying, "This person just doesn't like me"

When facing this type of generalized disapproval, the most productive efforts you can make to improve the situation include actions such as:

- Selectively disclosing some personal aspects of yourself that might help the other person see you as "a real person," gently challenging any of the biases they currently hold of you

- Asking a peer who might have similar qualities as you (i.e., a female engineer under 35 years of age) to see if the other person treats your peer the same way. The peer may be able to validate your experiences (which can help reduce your personal discomfort), or, this peer may be able to offer you suggestions about approaches they have found helpful in handling conflicts with this individual

Conflicts Involving Displaced Anger

Displaced anger is misdirected anger that is directed at you by another person, when in reality the other person should be directing the anger at the person who "caused" the anger.

In essence, this person has become angry over some other event in his or her life (an argument with their partner, frustration with a failing project they are leading, or a reprimand from their manager) and they are passing that anger on to you, often with little awareness of what they are doing.

You may be the recipient of this type of anger when you notice that:

- The individual is angry over small or inconsequential aspects of your work, and is displaying an intensity of anger that you think is way out of proportion to the issue being discussed

- At the first encounter with this person on any certain workday (in person, on the phone, etc.) you observe nonverbal indicators (facial expressions, an edge to their voice, a cognitive distraction, etc.), suggesting that something is already bothering him, and it is not related to anything you have done

The most productive approaches for dealing with displaced anger involve your:

- Giving this person a chance (at the start of your meeting) to externalize some of the displayed anger. An example of a statement that relates to this point is: "Mark, how is the day going so far...? It looks like you've had a really demanding morning already."

This type of question allows Mark an opportunity to pause, realize that he is already upset about some issue that does NOT involve you, and provides him a space to vent some of his feelings about the other subject before starting to dialogue with you. You can consider:

- Taking cues from Mark about how much he wants to "vent" about the subject. Be a listener, but don't probe too much, and follow his lead about when he appears to want to move onto other subjects

- Actively redirecting him to his current meeting with you, while subtly helping him realize that he is really not angry with you. An example of a statement that achieves this goal is: "Mark, that sounds like a very frustrating situation...would you like to take a few minutes to catch your breath and grab a cup of coffee before you and I start our meeting?"

The Triangulating Individual

An angry individual can also express his or her anger through "triangulation." This is a process in which anger is expressed indirectly. Rather than the person being direct with you about the anger, he or she shares it with a third party (their manager, or your manager, or another stakeholder) with the hope of putting indirect pressure on you to take a certain action, or possibly as a means of damaging your credibility and reputation.

You may be dealing with triangulated anger when you:

- Experience this person as cool, aloof, and unresponsive to you for no obvious reason

- You begin hearing rumblings of dissatisfaction from other stakeholders

- Your manager announces to you that you have a problem with this individual, and you are caught unaware

As a rule of thumb, the triangulating person tends to be someone who is indirect and has trouble with situations involving direct conflict. Hence, they distance themselves from the target of their anger (in this case, you!) by passing the anger through a third party, whom they hope will get the message to you. In extreme situations, this triangulating behavior can be very manipulative.

The most successful strategies for working with a triangulating individual involve:

- Your frequently checking in with them to sample their satisfaction/dissatisfaction with your work product

- Using open-ended questions (such as "Karen, can you describe what you're liking about the work to date, as well as what areas need attention?")

- Avoiding closed ended questions ("Karen, are things going well on the project?") because it is too easy for the triangulator (who by definition tends to be indirect) to answer with evasive answers in order to avoid possible conflict

Here is a brief overview of each of these three types of anger, along with suggestions on how to handle each type:

Personality-based conflict (You have the experience of just "not being liked" by the other person):

- Let the other person see additional sides of you

Conflict from displaced anger (Other person's anger seems disproportionate to the issues at hand):

- Help the other person "blow off some steam" before the two of you get down to work

Conflict from triangulation (You start to indirectly hear that someone has an issue with you):

- Actively and regularly seek out the other person to get feedback on "how you are doing"

Consider this typology of three types of conflict when working to develop an understanding on why the stakeholder is angry, but keep in mind that one should not view these three categories of sources of anger too mechanistically.

In reality, conflict anger may include various combinations of all three sources described above. Use this typology not to find the "true" source of the anger, but rather as a grounding for you to consider when beginning to craft some initiatives that might reduce the amount of anger coming your way.

Eight Interpersonal Approaches for Managing Conflict

I have found eight (often subtle) interpersonal approaches that are very useful for effective conflict management. These skills are listed below, and are then described in greater detail.

- Open-ended questions
- Active listening
- "Yes, and..." statements
- Application of silence
- Willingness to try the unusual
- Application of self-disclosure and "teaching"
- Consider the personal style of the other party
- Apply a space-value-closure approach

Open-Ended Questions

As the name suggests, open-ended questions are questions that you ask that cannot be answered with a yes or a no. During conflicts, these questions are very helpful in drawing the other person out and hopefully hearing some ideas or points that you did not hear during the periods where you may have been making statements, as compared to asking questions.

At their best, open-end questions create a non-judgmental atmosphere where you are seeking data, ideas, opinions, or concepts from the other person, so that these ideas can be literally or metaphorically written on the white board for further consideration.

Open-ended questions are extremely useful when the parties are locked into firm positions, and tensions are at high levels. At these times, an open-ended question can serve as a means of reducing the tension in the room, giving both parties more "space" within which they can look for movement. (The idea of "space" is developed further in this chapter when I present a very simple, but elegant model for conflict management that is known as the space-value-closure method).

Active Listening

A natural partner for open-ended questions is the skill of using active listening. This communication skill involves your listening closely to what the other person is saying (without feeling any need to say whether you agree or disagree with what they are saying), and then finding a way to communicate back to them what you think they are saying. Next, you can ask them for confirmation about whether or not you correctly captured both the essence and detail of what they just said.

Active listening helps you slow down the prosecution of your argument and really try to see if the other party is saying something that you may not have previously grasped. Too often during conflict, there is a tendency for the "listener" to not really be listening, but instead, silently formulating their rebuttal before the other party has put a period after their last sentence.

As with open-ended questions, active listening helps bring to the surface views and ideas that may have been missed earlier, and is especially helpful during those tense log-jam moments where all progress appears stuck, and both parties are reduced to repeating their previously articulated positions—and then repeating them again and again.

"Yes, and..." Statements

Often during conflicts, you may find it helpful to acknowledge the other person's point, but you also may desire to not get stuck on that point (especially if you believe that point is counterproductive towards moving forward). The "yes, and..." phrase helps you accomplish both of those goals.

For example, let's assume the other person says something unproductive, like the following:

> "Sue, you and your team are always late on your deliverables."

To this type of challenging statement, you do not want to take the bait and get stuck debating the accuracy of the statement, or maybe even try to defend yourself about some actual deadlines that were missed. Either of those responses will keep you immersed in a negative exchange.

Instead, you can use a "yes, and..." statement that allows the other person to feel "heard" while also keeping the conversation moving in a positive direction, as compared to one of fault finding. Here's an example of such a "yes, and..." statement:

> "Mike, yes, I do understand that we have been late at times—I agree. And what do you think we all can do to reduce the chance of that happening again?"

Application of Silence

Paradoxically, silence, when used artfully, is a powerful tool for managing a conflict situation. Silence in response to the angry stakeholder helps dissipate the anger because:

- The "silent" space between you and the other person allows the anger to fall to the floor

- Silence, when accompanied by strong eye contact, tells the angry individual "I see you are angry, I am not going to engage you on this anger, and I am going to pursue a more productive path when you are ready."

Use silence selectively, because its overuse may create the impression that you:

- Agree with what the other person is saying

- You are a passive individual

Your Willingness to Try the Unusual

Your willingness to be unpredictable in your comments and behavior can result in approaches that can break an unproductive conflict cycle, and catch the attention of the other party in a way that opens up new directions for the two of you to take.

For example, some aggressive individuals have become accustomed to this pattern: they come at you with verbal aggression, you sit through what they are saying and try to make sense of it, or you debate their assertion, or you do something else that they have come to expect from you.

However, if you respond in an unpredictable manner in the face of their anger, you may be able to catch them off guard, which can result in their slowing down, and reducing their angry output.

Here is an example of responding in an unpredictable manner:

- Rather than sit in your chair and let the team member communicate towards you in an angry and aggressive manner (which has been their pattern to date), you stand up during the discussion, move to the whiteboard, and start listing the other person's concerns

This process of physically altering the space between the two of you often catches the other person by surprise, interrupting their angry presentation, and assists them in being more open to approaching the discussion in a different manner.

Application of Self-Disclosure and "Teaching"

When you are involved in a conflict with a person who will be present in your life for an extended period of time, it can be helpful to casually teach the other person about your preferred approaches for managing conflict. An example of a statement that involves this concept of teaching is:

> "Michael, I really appreciated your willingness to take a break this morning and let each of us catch our breath. I find that those pauses during conflicts assist me in gathering my thoughts and reflecting on what I think I can do differently in working with you on our disagreement."

Thus, you are coaching the other person about what works best for you when conflict or anger arises. Granted, this form of self-disclosure and coaching is not always possible or appropriate. However, it can have significant benefits when applied deftly.

Keep it as an option, particularly in your relationships with long-term stakeholders with whom you need to have a significant business and personal investment in addressing emerging conflict situations.

Consider the Personal Style of the Other Person

As mentioned earlier in the book, the concept from psychology of individual differences can be a valuable approach to follow when you want to tailor an approach to another person, in this case the approach being in service of communicating with the person so as to best manage the conflict.

I find that the individual differences model of the Myers-Briggs Type Indicator (MBTI) has much to offer when considering how to manage a conflict. Below, I offer my thoughts about using the MBTI to craft the optimal approach for approaching an individual during a conflict.

- **Extrovert:** This person wants to think out loud about the problem and the possible solutions.

- **Introvert:** Give this individual a chance to "think about it" and get back to you at a later time.

- **Sensing:** Provide this person with tangible examples of the problem or issue.

- **Intuition:** This stakeholder wants to address any current issue in terms of broader considerations or future trends.

- **Thinking:** Develop with this individual an approach to managing the conflict that appears logical and rational.

- **Feeling:** Someone with this preference wants the approach to "feel right," considering emotion and morale.

- **Judging:** With this person, work towards an orderly approach that results in rules and guidelines.

- **Perceiving:** This stakeholder will not want to rush into a solution, and is willing to keep options open.

Using these MBTI guidelines, you can literally cut-and-paste a best practices approach for managing a conflict with a specific individual.

For example, if you are having conflict with someone you perceive as having an MBTI style of ESTJ (please refer back to Chapter 2 for behavioral cues for identifying MBTI styles), you can see that the implied optimal approach for managing a conflict with this person might look like the following:

Extravert → Think out-loud with this person about possible approaches

Sensing → in a manner that is tangible and concrete

Thinking → in which you present logical and rationale paths forward

Judging → that reflect a desire to reduce future conflicts

Apply a "Space- Value-Closure" Process Approach

Killen and Murphy (2003), writing about the MBTI, offer a very simple and powerful process model for addressing a conflict. For them, working through a conflict requires that both parties *create additional space* in which they can navigate, work hard to *identify the value that each party* brings to the discussion, then *define the basis for closure*, and once a conflict is managed, *try not to re-visit it* unless required.

Examples of each of these three processes include:

Create space by:

- Taking time-outs

- Asking open-ended questions to bring to the surface new ideas

- Meeting in a different physical location, or adopting a different conceptual posture for addressing the topic

Identify the value of each party's view by:

- Each party listing their points on a whiteboard, without debate or comment from the other party

- Assuming that each party has at least one or two legitimate points to be integrated

- After both parties list their individual points, "circle" the points that both parties can agree upon

Define the basis for determining conflict closure:

- Often, we become involved in conflict interactions without taking the time to stop and define the parameters that each party can agree on that will tell both parties when they have arrived at closure for the conflict. Therefore, be sure to pause and identify the points or metrics that will tell both of you when the conflict is managed

- Unless serious risk issues surface after a decision has been reached (such as safety or quality issues, or issues involving significant resource waste), leave the decision alone, and fight the tendency to re-visit the topic with an even better idea after a good night's sleep

The three-step process of the space-value-closure model provides you with a clear path to follow. However, remember that in most conflicts, this three step process does not unfold in a neat, linear manner. More often, these processes are experienced and achieved through an iterative manner, revisiting each stage as necessary.

Having said that, I want to emphasize that I still find the space-value-closure model to be one of beauty and efficacy. Additionally, I have had many projects managers tell me that its three tangible stages are immensely helpful in charting a new course when conflict is present within cross-cultural settings (where it is frequently difficult to know where to start, given the complexities of cultural overlays).

Applying the Thomas-Kilmann Conflict Mode Model (TKI)

Kenneth Thomas and Ralph Kilmann (2005) have crafted a model for addressing conflict that stresses the importance of developing competency in each of five conflict resolution approaches. This approach has been very well received over the years in my project management people skills seminars. In these settings, attendees have spoken about appreciating the specificity of the approaches, plus the idea that there is no one correct way to manage a conflict.

Indeed, the TKI model posits that you as leader need to have an adequate level of skill in each of five approaches to managing a conflict. Unfortunately, we generally prefer to use the one approach around which we have the greatest comfort, even using this approach in situations where it is not the optimal approach. Thus, the model suggests that we also need to have knowledge about *what approach works best in what setting.*

Thomas and Kilmann's model for managing a conflict includes the following five approaches: Avoiding, Compromising, Accommodating, Collaborating, and Competing. (These approaches have been described in greater detail by Flannes and Levin, 2005). Here is an overview of the five approaches:

Avoiding

The Avoiding approach is best used when the issue at hand is not that important or emergent, and for whatever reason, you desire to not address the situation at that time.

In essence, in using Avoiding, you make a conscious decision that says that you would rather "pick your battles," possibly because you do not currently have enough information about the topic, or you are feeling cognitively distracted and would rather address the issue after a good night's sleep. Here are sample statements that reflect an Avoiding approach to managing a conflict:

- "Yes, that's a possibility…let's think more about that and talk again."

- "I realize that's an issue….what's most important to talk about today?"

Keep in mind that if Avoiding is over-used in situations where it is not appropriate (such as where the other person is legitimately angry about something that you did or did not do), you run the risk of being seen as passive and unresponsive, possibly failing in your role as leader.

In all situations when using Avoiding, it is crucial to give the other party a specific time and place when you *will* be available to re-visit the issue. Without establishing such a re-visit time, you run the risk of issues remaining open and unaddressed.

Compromising

You can use Compromising when you and the other party both need to achieve something tangible in managing the conflict, and when the conflict is one in which compromising ("meeting in the middle") does not result in diminished quality or a risk management problem.

An example of a conflict where Compromising could be appropriate is when there is a disagreement regarding capital resources (for example, you want six engineers for your project, the sponsoring executive wants to give you four, and the two of you end up settling on five).

Examples of statements reflective of a Compromising approach to managing a conflict include:

- "I need to have Bill work on this project. If Bill works on this project, what would you need from me in order to cover your other responsibilities?"

- "OK, I can move up the completion date, but I'll need you to alter the specifications or change the level of resources I'm getting."

If you over-use Compromising in managing a conflict, you may be perceived as not confident or not very knowledgeable as leader. Conversely, if you under-use Compromising, you can be perceived as too rigid and unyielding.

Accommodating

The approach of Accommodating is often difficult to conceptualize and exemplify. At its core, this approach is useful when a conflict begins to surface between you and another person, but you personally have no strong feelings about how the situation should be addressed, while the other party does hold strong feelings.

Such a situation could be one where the other person has strong feelings about where the team off-site meeting should be held, but you personally don't really care where it is held. By using Accommodating, you in essence tell the person that whatever they want to do on this situation is fine, and you will support their decision. Often, the use of Accommodating enables you to win some political points with the other person, due to their perceiving you as both trusting and flexible. Here are some examples of Accommodating statements:

- "That's fine… we can do it your way on this."

- "What can I do for you on this issue to make it not a problem anymore?"

However, relying too much on the Accommodating approach results in your being seen as a passive and overly hands-off leader, while under-use can create the perception of you as always having to have it your way, even on insignificant issues.

Collaborating

Collaboration is the most interactive and win-win oriented method to use in managing a conflict. This approach involves you and the other person taking the time to think out loud about a myriad of possibilities and solutions, with the goal of creating an approach that is better than the proposed approach promulgated initially by either of you.

Collaborating should only be used when the issue is of enough importance to warrant both parties devoting significant amount of time to the effort. Also, to use this conflict management approach, you need to perceive that both you and the other party have appropriate levels of expertise on the topic, thus making the time spent together a worthy allocation of human capital.

Below are phrases and sample statements reflective of your taking a Collaborative approach:

- "Sounds like we both have some good ideas. How can we integrate them together?"

- "I hadn't thought of that point before, and I like it. How can we make it work with some of the other ideas that I mentioned earlier?"

Competing

Competing is the most assertive—and possibly aggressive—of the five approaches. You want to use this approach in managing a conflict only when you perceive that the other party is wrong about a crucial aspect of the project (a waste of resources, or a safety issue, or a major quality issue), and you believe you need to keep this negative event or decision from happening, almost at all costs.

Use this approach sparingly. You must be willing to "step on toes," due to the seriousness of the possible consequences. Examples of Competing statements that you can use include:

- "Bill, I realize that you want to do it your way, but I can't OK that change. We'll have to keep proceeding along our current path."

- "Bill, you don't seem to be hearing me. We can't change directions, and we're sticking to the original plan!" (*Increasing your intensity to make the point*)

- "Bill, when you're the boss, sitting in this chair, you can do it your way! Until then, we're going to follow my plan." (*Using humor to defuse a possibly tense situation*)

Again, use Competing only when it is absolutely necessary, as its overuse creates the image of you as too authoritarian. Additionally, overuse also results in less creativity in your team, because such an aggressive style can create a compliance mentality among your team members, as individuals may want "to just go along in order to get along."

In summary, these five Thomas-Kilmann approaches are very effective in managing conflicts, due to their specificity and their application to different types of conflict settings. Thomas and Kilmann have created a self-assessment instrument (Consulting Psychologist Press: cpp-db.com) that one can take to receive a formal description of their preferred approach to conflict management, but you can still use the techniques without actually taking the self-assessment.

What Are Your Personal Impediments or Triggers During a Conflict?

Each leader has his or her own set of behaviors and attitudes that help or hinder a conflict management process. Here are a number of attitudes, behaviors, or external variables that can hinder your ability in conflict management.

Attitudes:

- Do you tend to ignore or deny the existence of a conflict?

- Do you tend to respond to a conflict in what I might describe as an overly positive approach, coming across as a cheerleader, inferring that if just everyone thinks positively, everything will work out just fine?

Problematic external variables:

- Do you find you are especially ineffective in conflict management when you are dealing with a certain type of person, such as someone who uses verbal aggression or triangulating communication to address the conflict? If so, keep this awareness very prominent in your awareness.

Your personal behaviors:

- Do you have a tendency to over-respond to a conflict, such as looking for the quick fix in order to reduce your discomfort?

- Do you get mired in over-utilizing one of the previously described five conflict approaches popularized by Thomas and Kilmann?

- Do you over-utilize one communication mode of exchanging conflict management communication (such as sending overly detailed emails), when a more casual phone call might be more effective?

These attitudes, external variables, and personal behaviors are just examples how you and everyone else can bring less functional approaches to any emerging conflict.

Your goal is one of knowing enough about yourself so that you enter a conflict management situation with an awareness of what you might bring that could make the situation better or worse.

Cross-Cultural Challenges and Models

A number of years ago, while preparing for a presentation in the United Kingdom, I discovered that the Myers-Briggs Type Indicator (MBTI) was available in three forms of the English language. Yes, *three* forms of English.

These English versions of the MBTI consisted of a version in "North American English," a second version in "United Kingdom English," and a third version in "European English."

Discovering the existence of these three English versions of the MBTI had a powerful influence on me. I realized that if there can be three versions, then the world must be a complicated collection of cultures, where language and communication subtleties run rampant, and few cultural assumptions can be taken for granted.

The scope of this book is not one of exploring cross-cultural variables in detail. However, there are some interesting research efforts taking place that are examining how culture influences the selection of conflict management tools. Additionally, there is work being done looking at how variables such as cultural individualism and collectivism can vary significantly when identifying conflict approaches among cultural subgroups.

Two pertinent research efforts will be presented below to give a flavor of the interesting trends in looking at project conflict management approaches within cultural frameworks.

Randeree and El Faramawy (2011) examined Islamic perspectives within projectized work groups. They note that conflict within an Islamic perspective is viewed as a normal and expected experience, and can become a positive experience if approached appropriately.

Specifically, Randeree and El Faramawy describe three conflict management approaches that they perceive as consistent with basic Islamic tenets. These three models are the proactive model, the SALAM model, and the S.N.T. model. Very brief descriptions of the three models are presented below:

Proactive Model

The proactive model is an offshoot of basic Islamic leadership principles, and it involves an active, step-oriented approach to surveying the perceptions of involved stakeholders ahead of expected changes, so that the resultant conflict or resistance to such changes are minimal.

The SALAM Model

The second approach presented by Randeree and El Faramawy, the SALAM model, involves a five step process leading stakeholders to a desired conflict-free conclusion. The steps in the SALAM model are as follows:

S=   State the views present in the conflict

A=   Obtain agreement among parties that a conflict does exist

L=   Listen for the differences among perspective and views

A=   Advise one another

M=   Minimize areas of disagreement that can lead to aggression or withdrawal

The S.N.T. Model

And finally, Randerre and El Faramawy offer the S.N.T. model, which is grounded in Islamic principles such as the search for the experiences of consultation, advice, and cooperation.

In summarizing their research on these three approaches to managing conflict, the authors note that their empirical work suggested that Western project managers would not feel any inherent discomfort should they apply any of the three approaches in their projectized work.

Another investigation illuminates an area of study that is looking at conflict management variances among cultural sub-groups. In their study, Riaz and Jamal (2012) examined how Pakistani sub-cultures might vary in approaches to managing conflict based upon their position along the individualistic-collectivist cultural continuum. They speculated that even within the macro Pakistani culture (which is collectivist in nature) there will be significant variances along the individualist-collectivist continuum in terms of how certain sub-groups approach conflict.

This work of Riaz and Jamal would seem to make the point we all should remember that even national cultural groups will have differences within sub-groups, and we should therefore refrain from making blanket generalizations about the conflict management approaches of the members of an individual nation state.

Other Research Trends

The research on conflict within projectized environments offers some interesting ideas and directions. Here are just a few examples, presented to give you an appreciation for the depth and complexity of the experience of conflict.

Frah, Lee, and Farh (2010) offer us some impressive findings on the impact of conflict during different project stages, and the resulting influence of conflict upon the team's creativity.

These researchers note that "task conflict" (defined as conflict regarding resources, decisions, and judgments—and not interpersonal conflicts) can improve team effectiveness and creativity, but only when it emerges in the early stages of a project.

Additionally, the level of task conflict should be moderate; higher levels of task conflict create the risk that conflict will become personalized. In general, it is better to manage your team so that interpersonal conflict is minimized, and if conflict is to be present, task or content conflict is much better.

Many other researchers writing on the topic of conflict in teams suggest that all forms of conflict are best addressed within a team culture noted for "psychological safety," which according to Bradley, Postlethwaite, Klotz, Hamdani, and Brown (2012) is "...the shared belief held by team members that the team is safe for interpersonal risk..."

New Theoretical Approaches

Innovative and creative conceptualizations about conflict management are being developed from a number of different perspectives. These efforts have in common the goal of creating sophisticated approaches to conflict management that rise above the level of seeing conflict improvement as merely a case of "negotiation" between stakeholders.

Thus, these innovative approaches to conflict management see the process not just as one of "reducing conflict," but rather as one of designing tools that can bridge conflict-creating chasms between stakeholders, so that knowledge transfer, especially in cross-national projects, proceeds with as few interruptions as possible.

One such approach to increasing knowledge sharing while minimizing conflict is described by DiMarco, Alin, and Taylor (2012), who speak of the benefits of creating "boundary objects." These authors describe boundary objects as design objects, models, and various specification documents that serve as *a meeting place* for virtual workers, where the boundary objects have enough plasticity to incorporate respective cultural influences of different individuals, but are also robust enough to integrate knowledge sharing across subgroups.

And finally, work is being done on the subject of "intractable conflict." Vallacher, Coleman, Nowak, and Wrzosinksa (2010) write about how intractable conflict can exist in dynamic systems even when all parties in the conflict can articulate that there is no logical reason or benefit for the perpetuation of the conflict.

While this work is directed more at the macro level, often towards the interactions of nation states, I nevertheless believe that it holds value even when considered on the team level.

Interestingly, Vallacher et al. state that competition for resources and the presence of ideological differences are not the main sources of conflict. Rather, they believe that intractable conflict emerges due to the thoughts, beliefs, and memories held by the key actors. Consequently, I believe that their work suggests that it is important for you as leader to create a team culture noted for optimism and the benefits of a mutually defined future focus, so that "intractable" gaps do not emerge between your team and other stakeholder groups.

Summary

Conflict management in enterprise settings is always complicated and difficult, and is especially so in projectized enterprise environments.

I have often found it helpful when approaching any task involving conflict to have a checklist that I can follow towards the goal of my having a starting place and at the least, a rudimentary sense of direction.

With that goal of having a checklist for the process of managing conflict, I offer Table 8.1 as a starting point for you to consider when you are addressing a conflict.

Table 8.1

Conflict Management Checklist

Questions to Ask Yourself	Action to Take	Action's Benefit
Is the conflict due to a *lack of information* with one of the parties?	Review the basic facts and details of the situation	Many lengthy conflicts can be avoided if you make sure each party has the correct information and facts
Have you adopted a *helpful mindset* for the conflict management?	Attempt to use your most effective communication skills and abilities: Manage, not resolve Focus on what you need Manage the relationship, not the person Watch for "traps"	You must have the most optimal mindset and outlook in place *before* you begin to address the content of the conflict
Are you employing, as appropriate, each of the 8 *interpersonal approaches*?	Employee a variety of approaches to create new possibilities	Reduces the risk that the process will stagnate
Do you need to use any of the 5 Thomas-Kilmann approaches?	Mix and match during the discussion, as needed	There is value in realizing that each of the 5 approaches may be appropriate at different points even within the *same* conversation
As the leader, do you bring any of your own *impediments or triggers* that can hamper progress?	Keep your awareness up, with attention being paid to how you personally may be slowing the progress	Self-knowledge of your weak spots helps you grow and develop (long-term) as well as manage conflicts (short-term)

Again, for me, I always find checklists helpful when addressing situations that may cause me anxiety and defensiveness. The checklist then serves as a guide that I follow in stepping into the uncomfortable situation.

Always keep in mind that conflict is both natural and desired, helping craft innovative solutions when managed with a steady hand. Actively address conflict situations, and be sure to focus on what you *need*, not what you *want*.

Chapter 9
Achieving Optimal Productivity and Well-Being in a Fast-Paced Technology Environment: A Win-Win Proposition

Mike Mombrea

Mike Mombrea's chapter describes an innovative approach he developed for working with high-functioning executives and technology professionals. He created this approach during his five-year tenure as the Employee Assistance Counselor for Optum Behavioral Solutions at the LifeConnections Health Center, a state-of-the-art integrated healthcare clinic in Silicon Valley, created by Cisco Systems for its employees and families. Mike's unique combination of hands-on, practical strategies ("mindfulness techniques") offers us a set of self-management tools we can use in managing the performance/personal challenges inherent in our working within today's 24/7 workplace mindset. Mike also gained perspectives on the 24/7 performance expectations during his tenure as Executive Vice-President of Account Services for ValueOptions, a leading company in the behavioral healthcare industry. Recently, Mike became the Employee Assistance Program Director for the San Francisco Giants baseball team.

Mike is a licensed Marriage & Family Therapist, and has a master's degree in Clinical Psychology from John F. Kennedy University and a master's degree in Political Science from the State University of New York at Buffalo. Mike may be reached at mombo109@gmail.com.

In this chapter, I present practices drawn from the world of neuroscience and mindfulness that will assist you in:

- Optimizing performance and your leadership potential

- Improving life balance

- Reducing emotional reactivity

- Gaining a greater sense of personal comfort and interpersonal satisfaction

I have served as a leader in a number of organizational settings, working as a Program Director in the non-profit sector and at the Vice-President level for a national behavioral healthcare organization within the corporate sector. I have also served as an employee assistance counselor working with a multicultural population found within a successful global technology corporation.

Supplementing my organizational experience, I have earned a master's degree in psychology and am licensed as a behavioral therapist.

Along the way, I have looked at the topic of leadership through these two windows: corporate leader and behavioral health therapist. As one can expect, such divergent world experiences offer a variety of views on leadership. What works, what doesn't? Who are the effective leaders, and how do they get that way?

In this chapter, I share resources that I believe contribute to both individual and organizational effectiveness.

Resources for Demanding Times

In recent years, I have concentrated my efforts on helping technology professionals achieve demanding performance goals while *also* maintaining a sense of emotional contentment and satisfaction.

As we know all too well, advances in technology have proved to be a double-edged sword. The capacity for 24/7 connectivity and the expansion of work schedules to accommodate global time zones have obliterated traditional work/life boundaries.

This 24/7 connectivity challenges leaders to optimize productivity while also developing creative approaches that support their health and well-being, as well as that of their employees, who are impacted by the stress associated with the blurring of work/life boundaries, which lead to a vulnerability to anxiety and depression.

My Approach Is Conducive to a Technology Mindset

Because a majority of high tech employees have a background in computer science and engineering, I present my work in a manner that is consistent with a technology/scientific mindset.

Specifically, I educate my clients about the mechanics of stress, with particular attention to the physiological manifestations on the cardiovascular, immune and gastrointestinal systems. Such a broad focus helps individuals see the impact that a 24/7 mindset has on their overall health.

This orientation about the mechanics of stress provides a context for my recommendations, which involve the employment of scientifically validated relaxation techniques that reduce stress by engaging the parasympathetic nervous system. (The parasympathetic nervous system supports the body's need for restoration, while increasing the capacity for concentration, and increased productivity).

In presenting my thoughts about resources for the performance challenges inherent within a 24/7 milieu, I cover the following topics in this chapter:

- Describe my experience in using an innovative, on-line "brain health" assessment/report, the WebNeuro, as a supplemental resource for identifying the presence of anxiety and depression within my clients (http://services. brainresource.com/webneuroreportreference)

- Introduce the concept of negativity bias[1] and its correlation with stress, anxiety and depression

- Describe the application of a mindfulness technique to reduce stress, anxiety and depression. (The term "mindfulness" refers to the ability to be fully aware and engaged in the present moment, in contrast to being preoccupied with the future or past)

How My Approach Works

I begin my work with technology professionals (many of whom are senior level leaders) by requesting they complete the WebNeuro online assessment. The WebNeuro assessment (as cited earlier) was devised by Brain Resources, Ltd. and involves the test taker's responses to self-report questions and participation in brain games to determine one's current level of behavioral and cognitive functioning. In suggesting the assessment, I advise my clients that the results of the assessment will help guide the direction of our work by providing us with a baseline of objective data pertaining to his or her current level of functioning.

During our second meeting, I review the assessment results with the client, focusing on areas of vulnerability and strength as revealed by the WebNeuro assessment. The driver of my approach is to examine assessment scores in a few very important subcategories, which include:

- Negativity Bias

- Anxiety

- Stress

- Depression

- Emotional Resilience

- Attention and Concentration

- Memory

I have found that such early access to the assessment results engages clients by identifying core issues, and by expediting our creating a collaborative, solution-focused approach.

One of the challenges in working with clients in an action-oriented, short-term, solution-focused setting is that *we often don't know what we don't know*. The WebNeuro assessment addresses this dilemma by providing valuable self-report feedback to the client. This information supplements my initial clinical impressions, sharpening my focus and strengthening our working alliance.

---

[1] The term Negativity Bias is derived from brain research demonstrating that humans are hard-wired for survival, making us acutely sensitized to danger or threat, and in the modern era, manifested in fears of job loss and failure (See *Buddha's Brain*, New Harbinger Publications, 2009, by Rick Hanson)

I have worked with over 600 individuals in this demanding technology environment. My observations from my work with these 600 individuals are summarized in Table 9.1

Table 9.1

Frequent Results from the WebNeuro Assessments of 600 Technology Professionals

Behavior, Cognitive, or Emotional Variable	Definition of this Variable	How Might This Variable Impact the Individual's Work Performance or Personal Balance?
Stress	Physical and emotional strain when demands exceed our ability to respond	Immune system compromised, high blood pressure, headaches, irritability, and impact on sleep
Anxiety	Feelings of worry, nervousness or unease related to an imagined or real future outcome	Inability to focus, a decrease in productivity, and physical exhaustion
Depression	Severe feelings of sadness, hopelessness and inadequacy	Emotional isolation, withdrawal, decrease in interpersonal effectiveness
Negativity bias	Hypersensitivity to danger or threat; the expectation of negative outcomes	Pessimism, the "cup half empty"

The Strong Impact of the Negativity Bias

Because the negativity bias is associated with the emotional control center of the brain, its role in contributing to our inner narrative is invisible (in the absence of conscious attention to the interplay between our emotions and thinking). The subjective experience of individuals with a strong negativity bias is that their feelings of inadequacy and fears of failure are out of their control.

For example, one individual with a high degree of negativity bias knew that her compensation was below her grade level for the position she held, but she had avoided approaching her manager for over a year because she was afraid that her request for an increase in compensation would be rejected and that she would feel humiliated.

After we discussed her fears (while also talking through the perceived risks involved in raising the issue with her manager), the client actively engaged her manager in the compensation discussion during her next performance review meeting.

The client described the discussion as almost "anticlimactic," suggesting that she had successfully applied various effective strategies. Indeed, she stated that her manager, who was relatively new in her position, agreed to address the issue with human resources.

Assisting Individuals in Restoring a Sense of Control

A key to helping such clients restore a sense of control is to teach them how to observe the thoughts and emotions associated with their stress, anxiety and depression.

To facilitate this process, I introduce a *mindfulness exercise* that increases one's ability to monitor the thoughts, emotions and physical sensations through a process of quiet self-reflection. The exercise involves sitting quietly for 10 minutes, non-judgmentally observing whatever thoughts arise.

As clients learn to observe the whirlpool of thoughts and emotions that surface, I instruct them to gently bring attention to their breathing. When I introduce this mindful awareness practice, I use analogies such as:

- Visualize your thoughts as clouds passing in the sky

- "Watch" your thoughts, rather than boarding the "I'm not-good-enough train"

As mindful awareness increases, individuals are able to more objectively focus on personal goals, relationship issues, and work challenges with an increased clarity and optimism. Additionally, people gradually begin to grasp the "perfect storm" paradox; that while advanced technologies have increased our capacity for connection, the accelerating pace of workplace demands often outpaces their ability to respond.

Prior to their application of mindfulness applications, many people typically report that their thoughts have tended to be focused in two directions:

1. Preoccupations with the future, and/or

2. Ruminations about the past

Clients who practice these mindfulness exercises regularly discover that quieting the mind creates the opportunity to *observe* rather than be *captivated* by the habitual nature of their distressing thoughts and emotions.

Here are frequent client-reported benefits of using the mindfulness practices:

- Reduced emotional reactivity, and increased patience with coworkers and family members

- Greater cognitive clarity and an increase in ability to prioritize

- Increased optimism, going from "the cup is half empty" to "the cup is half full" perspective

- Reduction in rumination on "the past" and less worrying about "the future"

- Increased levels of personal awareness and acceptance, along with a decrease in negative self-judgment

Presented below are two case examples that illustrate how I employ my approach to achieve positive outcomes in reducing the symptoms of depression, stress and anxiety.

A High-Level Global Project Executive

This individual was a 42-year-old, married male with two young children. He expressed concern that his level of stress had increased over a three-year period, as reflected by:

- An increasing level of irritability
- Conflict in his marriage
- Dissatisfaction in his work as a Senior Director

He shared that he had been assigned to a major project in Asia, a project that had a high degree of visibility. He had initially been reluctant to take this position, which turned out to be unsuccessful. He conveyed that the relocation of his family to Asia had been extremely stressful for his wife and two children, in part because the project had required extensive travel for him. He added that although there were many positive aspects of the experience, it still had taken a toll on him and his family.

Here is what he and I learned when we looked at his WebNeuro scores. He had:

- An acute level of Stress
- A marked deficit in the category of Attention and Concentration

As we discussed his assessment results, he told me that he did not like feeling frustrated and angry, and expressed concern that he was alienating his wife and children. He also said he felt estranged from his senior colleagues, even though he was now assigned to a new project and was receiving positive feedback. In response to my questions about his current level of distress, he expressed feeling that he failed on his recent assignment while simultaneously feeling angry with his senior colleagues for holding him accountable for the project's failure.

As the client began practicing the mindfulness exercise, he noticed that:

- As his mind slowed down and his body relaxed, he became less irritable
- His internal narrative of self-criticism (which was fueling his irritability) gradually decreased

As we continued to explore his priorities, he identified that improving his relationship with his wife and children was very important, due to the damage he felt he had done over the last three years. The first change he made was to devote 30 minutes every morning to being with his wife, checking in about the day ahead, and how they were doing with each other and with their children.

The second issue he wanted to address was related to his work and relationship with his colleagues. Interestingly, this leader asked me if I thought it would be in his interest to work on improving those relationships. My response was to encourage him to reflect on whether his desire to improve the relationships with his colleagues derived from his insecurity, or a genuine desire to connect with them in a more positive way.

After contemplating this question, he decided there was no need to prove himself to individuals he "did not trust," stating, "They were willing to throw me under the bus." He conveyed that he would be best served by letting go of his anger, viewing what happened as a learning experience and moving on.

Over the time we worked together, he reported that the meditation exercise had been a "life saver." He stated that his life had been falling apart, and that he was now practicing the exercise daily and prioritizing his time to be consistent with his commitment to his family. In our final meeting, he informed me that he accepted a senior position at a leading edge high-tech company.

Several months later, he contacted me to share that he was thrilled with his new position and that his relationship with his wife and family were going extremely well. Increasing his self-awareness through the mindfulness practice empowered him to sort out his thoughts and feelings, identify his priorities, and then to make changes consistent with his personal values and career goals.

An Accomplished Mother Who Did Not "Feel Successful"

This 40-year-old professional presented as emotionally overwhelmed, exhibited by feelings of anxiety, irritability, intermittent panic attacks, headaches and sleep difficulties.

She had moved with her family from China to the U.S. when she was quite young. She completed her college degree in the U.S., subsequently married and had two children.

During the initial phases of her counseling, we saw that her WebNeuro scores showed high levels of stress and anxiety, as well as severe depression.

When I shared the WebNeuro depression score with her, she broke down and expressed that she was feeling so distressed that she had begun thinking that life was not worth living. She revealed that she had always been singularly focused on academic achievement and financial security, values that her parents emphasized from early childhood. She stated that although she and her husband were financially secure, she never felt successful. She went on to say that even her decision to have children was to fulfill an expectation, and that she felt like she was "a failure as a parent."

What added to her distress was her lack of control over how overwhelmed and negative she was feeling about herself. In our review of her WebNeuro scores, she expressed relief that her distress was validated "in black and white" and stated, "I have always felt like I was never good enough."

As our work continued, I found different ways to suggest that we all can learn to question what we have internalized by cultivating the ability to observe our disturbing thoughts without being "hooked" by them. To assist in that specific goal, I walked her through a mindfulness exercise (which she recorded on her iPhone) that encouraged her to:

- Observe her thoughts, feelings and physical sensations without trying to change anything

- Gently focus her attention on her breathing

As I guided her through the exercise, I informed her that the activity of her mind would "intrude" again and again, and that when she noticed this happening, she should simply bring her attention back to her breath.

I encouraged her to practice the exercise daily between our meetings. During the course of our work, I also recommended several books and CDs that reinforced the benefits of observing the mind's activity. Over a six-month period (meeting with her initially weekly, and then gradually decreasing our meetings to monthly), I found that her anxiety and stress returned to normal levels, and her depression scores improved from acute to mildly symptomatic. Additionally, she reported that she was now able to monitor her habitual pattern of negative thoughts and feelings (her negativity bias) without "blaming" herself.

She also made a number of significant changes in how she *structured* her schedule. She now takes time off every week to volunteer at her son's Kindergarten class without feeling guilty that she is ignoring her work. She also terminated a business venture that was taking time away from her family. Importantly, she went on her first vacation in years where she didn't work during her time off.

Over time, she remarked that she previously had been unaware that her happiness was about the ability to *enjoy herself in the moment,* rather than chasing goals that she never felt she could reach. When I asked her what was generally different for her, she conveyed that she now had the tools to work on her issues.

My Reflections on the Needs in the Workplace

When I reflect on my experience in the variety of settings in which I have worked, the most conspicuous oversight I have noticed in these settings is the lack of attention paid to *the impact of our internal experience on organizational and individual effectiveness.* Our inward experience has been deemed off limits or irrelevant, in favor of a very strong emphasis that is traditionally placed on objective measures of productivity.

However, I believe that it is very important to focus on the personal aspect of leadership. In a recent conversation with a senior manager, he shared that one of his first line managers approached him one day and asked, "How do you deal with all of the stress at your level?"

The senior manager responded that it was paying attention to the human element that helped him the most. In elaborating on his response with me, he stated that talking about goals, strategy and the technical side of things really didn't help when his organization was under pressure.

He shared that empathizing with the people reporting to him, listening to their concerns, offering encouragement and reinforcing that they are *all in it together* made the biggest difference. He stated that it was very important to be honest with his team and his superiors about his concerns and limitations, so that mid-course corrections could be made.

And finally, he informed me that applying the various mindfulness techniques had increased his self-awareness, and had helped him maintain perspective on what is most important in his work and personal relationships.

Be True to Yourself

The business world would benefit from considering the famous line out of Shakespeare's *Hamlet*, "To thine own self be true," as a wake-up call to address the well-documented toll that stress, anxiety and depression have on the emotional well-being of the work force, as well as the bottom line.

I believe that there are a number of ways to address these issues and goals. Personally, my best description of these practices is captured below:

- The practice of mindful awareness empowers us to identify our self-limiting beliefs and to eliminate conditioned patterns of thinking that undermine our capacity to flourish at work and home.

Self-Reflection: It Is Crucial

I would like to conclude the chapter by offering a number of big-picture, future-oriented perspectives.

I believe the most critical evolutionary imperative for leaders at the present time is the need for genuine self-reflection. How we think and feel and our capacity for connection with colleagues have a direct impact on how effectively we handle our responsibilities.

The Importance of Attending to the Subjective

There are precious few work contexts in which people have opportunities to discuss and express the subjective aspects of their experience (relating to "who they are" and what they value most). In most work environments, actively encouraging time for contemplation and opportunities for open dialogue as a critical aspect of the business at hand would be considered anathema to the "ethic" of productivity.

The acceleration of personal, social, organizational and political crises is evidence that current world views, often intellectually dressed-up versions of "the good guys versus the bad guys," will not serve humanity in meeting the evolutionary objective of survival.

We ignore at our peril the need to honor the importance of our "inner environment." I believe that a strong focus on the inner world becomes a strategy for promoting the health of individuals, families, organizations, social networks and political communities.

The Survival Imperative

A focus on our "inner environment" should no longer be viewed as a conversation reserved for those interested in identifying the criteria for creating utopian communities. The rapid pace of technological growth, in addition to its myriad advantages, has created stressors requiring a level of self-discipline that will allow us to view with clarity the self-destructive path we are on.

For the first time, leaders in the business community must begin to marshal corporate resources to integrate the value of self-awareness and mindfulness practices. This focus will assist in the process of achieving deeper levels of individual and organizational integrity and will form the core of our emerging business enterprises as well as the foundation for a more optimal society.

Chapter 10
Reflections on Leading:
My Journey, My Learnings

Larry Butler

Larry Butler has had a successful career serving as the Senior Human Resource officer for a number of organizations in both the private and public sectors. The industries in which he has worked include universities, banking, behavioral health care, and technology. Over his career, Larry has witnessed the behavior of leaders at all levels of an organization, noting the personal qualities and behaviors of the most effective leaders. In addition to his corporate leadership roles, he has worked as an executive coach and seminar leader, as well as a licensed Marriage and Family Therapist. In this chapter, Larry shares his ideas on what constitute the core competencies of good leaders, while also sharing valuable tips on how you can best manage your evolving career. Larry resides in Piedmont, CA, with his wife, Sue. Larry can be reached at larrybutler1940@gmail.com.

Leadership. We hear this word daily, applied to almost all aspects of life. But defining what constitutes leadership is a daunting task.

In this chapter, I take an experiential approach in describing leadership, sharing with you what I have personally learned from my leadership experiences—both the good and the bad.

Additionally, I will share with you a model of human behavior that I found to be extremely helpful when I was positioned as a leader. Being able to define and articulate your own model of human behavior is crucial, because such belief systems serve as the foundation for all we do as leaders.

Also in this chapter are the results of recent informal research I have conducted. I asked 49 leaders (drawn from the ranks of CEOs of billion-dollar companies to leaders in the fields of social service) two questions about how they view leadership. Their replies were fascinating to me, and I hope they will be useful to you.

One crucial aspect of being a leader, an aspect that does not get enough attention and focus, is the concept of how *you* manage *your* career. I also address this topic in the chapter. No one else will manage your career for you, and the more skills you have in this area, the better you will be able to perform in the short run, as well as being "ready" for the moment when you realize you want to pursue a new opportunity.

And finally, I end the chapter with personal reflections on my individual leadership journey. I have had many wonderful experiences in leadership, but I have also paid a price.

This last section addresses my thoughts on how to work towards crafting more work/life balance when serving in demanding leadership roles.

Not *Another* Book on Leadership!

Over the last thirteen years, Steven Flannes and I have presented seminars throughout the United States and Canada, as well as the UK, Poland, and Ukraine.

Frequently, during our travels to and from these events, or over dinner, we would share perceptions of what each of us thought constituted "good leadership." As you can expect, our definitions of "leadership" took many forms and shapes during these fluid exchanges.

And so, when Steve asked me to write a chapter in his book on the subject of leadership, I quickly agreed, but soon found myself thinking the following:

- The word "leadership" is now used so often I believe it has become almost meaningless.

- I hear the word so frequently, it goes in one ear and out the other.

Hopefully, in this chapter, I will present my thoughts on leadership in a way that presents the concept in a different manner, that manner being *a set of values based upon personal experience*, as compared to a more sterile listing of research-identified skill sets.

Why *Me* as a Commentator on Leadership?

I've had a fairly unique career in my life, and therefore have had the opportunity to observe many leaders in a variety of circumstances. My work experiences have included:

- Large financial service companies

- Aerospace companies

- Technology organizations

- Utilities

- Start-ups in technology and health care

- Community mental health

- Academic institutions

- Healthcare organizations

Though I spent most of my career in human resource positions, I have also had sales, marketing, consulting and operational roles. Additionally, I was a practicing clinician as a licensed Marriage and Family Therapist while also serving on a number of boards in both the private and public sectors.

Early Beginnings

I grew up in the Chicago area where I attended college and graduate school. In the late 1960s I was employed by University of Illinois-Chicago. My position included working with the "activist-radical" student groups on campus, as well as the African-American community on the West Side of Chicago, helping the university relate to this neighborhood.

I then worked for the First National Bank of Chicago, where I ended up running all management and executive recruiting, as well as training and development. My next assignment involved a move to the San Francisco Bay Area, where I was head of Human Resources for The Bank of California (now Union Bank of California).

After the bank, I worked for an executive search firm in Silicon Valley and then went back to evening school for a master's degree in psychology. While attending graduate school, I consulted to aerospace, health care, banking, and outplacement companies.

I soon became head of human resources at PeopleSoft (now Oracle), and from there head of human resources and facilities at RightWorks, a technology start-up. In winding down my corporate career, I have continued to teach in the project management field. I also helped found and lead tbhe Oakland Police Foundation.

Quite an interesting variety of settings, and I enjoyed each one.

The Importance of "Situation" on Being Seen as a "Success" as Leader

Before I say more, I want to share with you my view about the importance of the following guideline:

- Leadership success is strongly determined by *situation.* The type of *current* situation a person is in often determines whether that person is considered a good leader or not.

Please consider the following question: Are you a "star" or a "bum?"

During my career, I've been considered a star a number of times. I've also been considered a bum a number of times. It's my belief that I wasn't all that different a person when I was considered a *star* vs. when I was considered a *bum*.

- But what *was* different was the situation I was in, and what was the correct fit for the role. At certain points in time, my fit for my role seemed to be close to a perfect match. And at that point in time, I was in the *star* category.

The importance of "situation" is also highlighted in this recent communication from a friend who has worked at the highest levels of a cabinet-level department within the Federal government:

"The attributes that make a person a good leader or manager will vary with the environment in which the person is working. A good leader in industry will not necessarily be a good leader in the government."

Over the years, I have found one approach to "modifying" the situation to favor my style. This leadership skill is the ability to *bend the job requirements* of a position to his or her skill set. And I believe all of us to greater or lesser degrees can use our skill sets to define our organizational roles. But, as I said previously, our position is also determined by forces external to us, and these forces are not necessarily in our control.

My Model for Looking at Human Behavior

Before I talk more directly about my thoughts about specific leadership skills, I want to first talk about a model of human behavior that I particularly like.

Why is having a model of human behavior important for a leader? That is a good question, with a simple answer:

- As a leader, you first need to be aware of *your* beliefs and values about human nature, because these variables will influence how you implement your leadership roles.

Now for the model. There are twelve key points in my model:

1. Everyone is born with an inner core of goodness.

   - We're born good. (Think of a newborn baby.) Everything that follows in this model is dependent on this assumption.

2. For most people, regardless of circumstances, it's possible to access this inner core of goodness, no matter how difficult it may seem.

3. As we grow and develop, our growth and personality are affected by heredity and our environment.

   - Some people are affected more strongly by their heredity—others by their environment—but how we end up at any point in time is a result of the interaction between the two.

4. As we grow, we develop filters and blinders through which we view the world.

   - These filters and blinders result from heredity and our interactions in the world.

5. If we are born with certain tendencies, or grow up in challenging environments, either one of these categories (heredity/environment) or a *combination of both can result in what others perceive to be very difficult personalities.*

6. With some people more than others, *the filters and blinders* not only obscure but *bury this inner core of goodness.* Though buried, it's still present and alive, and can be accessed, as difficult as it may seem.

7. *How we think determines how we feel, which determines how we behave.* So, to work on your leadership behavior, first work on modifying how you *think* about the issues.

8. Because people are born good, and they carry this inner core of goodness (no matter how covered it may be by the filters and blinders described above). *People are doing the best they can (at any point in time), given who they have become.*

9. And if people are doing the best they can (as unpleasant as that behavior may be), *we need not take their behavior personally.*

   - This is a key point, not only with individuals but with nations as well—we have a strong inclination to take behavior personally and react accordingly. When we take behavior personally, we either react or shut down.

10.   *Not taking behavior personally is very difficult to do*, especially in the heat of the moment, regardless of how well you understand and believe in this model.

11.   But if we can step back a bit and change how we think about the person's (or nation's) behavior and not take it personally, *we can also change how we feel about that person, and perhaps most importantly, how we behave towards that person.*

12.   By not taking behavior personally, we can step back from the moment and look at our situation in a cool and more rational manner rather than a heated, impulsive manner.

A Simple Model to Conceptualize, But Difficult to Apply

I firmly believe in my model of human behavior, having seen it serve me well in a number of complex business and interpersonal situations. However, it is often very difficult to implement!

I have embraced the principles of this model for approximately twenty years. It has been useful to me when I have been able to step back from the immediacy of a situation and remind myself about the principles of the model. But stepping back is not always easy.

- *Caveat*: Remember, it's always easier to apply the practices cited in the model when you are not in the heat of the moment. When you feel pressure, it's always more difficult to step back and apply these steps to your actions and behaviors. To me, it's important to take small steps in applying some of these practices, and it's most easily done in non-pressurized situations.

As an example of the usefulness *and* the difficulty in applying this model, I'd like to cite a personal example:

Recently, I had an interaction with a professional services firm that I have used for over twenty years. In reviewing the services they provide to me, they stated that I needed to make some modifications to my service package that would increase my costs by thousands of dollars. (During my twenty-year relationship with this organization, this was the first time I had been told that such costly changes needed to be made).

I became emotionally involved. Soon, I was irate with all parties who were involved, and I immediately began looking for a new organization with whom I could work.

Before long, others in my network started telling me that this really was a good service provider, but I wasn't listening. I was just too angry.

Gradually, I began to step back a bit back. I worked on *modifying the way I thought about the individuals* who were involved. By changing how I thought about the others, *my feelings started to shift*, and I then notice that *my behavior also changed some.*

I had been clearly *taking their behavior too personally*. But, by gradually trying to think that *the others were doing the best they could*, given the various limitations of their roles, I could look at the situation differently.

Not only could I feel myself letting go of my anger, I also found *I could think more clearly about this situation*. Going forward, I now realize that I don't need to be so personally involved. I can distance myself from the emotional side of any further situations, but still be involved with what is best for my interests.

My key point here is this:

- It's really difficult to think clearly when you are emotionally reacting to a situation, no matter how much practice you've had.

But though it's difficult, it's also possible to step away from the situation and look at it in a different light—one that permits you to be more effective in dealing with it. And by effective, I mean not just reducing your own stress level, but also permitting you to deal positively with the situation you are facing.

Change and Pain

As the above scenario indicates, I needed to change my mindset and behavior. Here are a few of my other thoughts on change.

- Change won't happen unless there is pain and/or anticipated pain. Without pain, or expected pain, there is no reason to change.

- If we are comfortable and satisfied with our present course and feel this present course will continue for as long as we can see, there is no reason to change anything.

Change is tough. If we are mostly comfortable, and even a bit uncomfortable, in our present state, there will always be powerful forces attempting to move us back to that prior state, should we have moved away from it.

People and organizations are the most comfortable in a steady state of doing things. When change occurs, we disrupt that steady state and its comfortable equilibrium, resulting in countervailing strong forces designed to return us to that old steady state.

The above thoughts explain why change is often difficult. It may appear logically easy, but there is a process at work attempting to take us back to the old and the comfortable. And that is why the pain or anticipated pain of doing nothing needs to be greater than doing nothing.

What Leaders Recently Told Me about Leadership

As I wrote more and more sections of this chapter, I started to believe that it might be valuable to survey friends of mine who are or were effective leaders, and to seek their views on leadership. To gather their impressions on what made good leaders, I asked them the following two questions:

- When you are in your leadership role, what are the two or three top qualities, capabilities, traits, etc. that you possess that make you an effective leader?

- What is one quality, capability, trait, etc., that you would like to improve upon in your role as a leader?

What I believe to be unique about the responses I received from these leaders is the very personal and self-disclosing nature of their answers. All the responders know me well. I believe these responses to be more honest and insightful than they otherwise would be, given the nature of our friendship. I made requests of 49 people, and 43 responded.

Those who answered occupy a wide variety of leadership positions and are a most diverse group, both in terms of ethnic and social backgrounds as well as types of leadership roles. Backgrounds of many of the responders are as follows:

Chief Executive Officers

- CEO and Chairman of a large multinational manufacturer with over 30,000 employees worldwide

- Founder and CEO of two Silicon Valley start-ups who is now a successful venture capitalist in India

- Founder and CEO of a company focusing on the blind population (he is blind)

- CEO of a healthcare company

- CEO and founder of a real estate development company

- CEO of an adventure travel company

- President and CEO of a professional human resources organization

- CEO of a chain of retirement homes

- CEO of a hotel chain

- CEO and chairman of a bank

- Founder of executive search firm

Entrepreneurs, Business Founders, and Managers

- Founder of a venture philanthropy fund in a major city, focusing on programs for the development of low income residents

- Founder and partner of a financial planning firm

- CPA and founder of a tax firm

- Winery owner

- Founder and partner of a financial services fund

- Artist/founder of an art studio dedicated to bringing art into local neighborhoods
- Healthcare consultant and founder/manager of two start-up healthcare organizations
- Founder/principle of two legal start-ups
- Senior manager of project management professionals
- Founders and partners of international and local venture capital firms

Government, Public Service, Education, and the Arts

- Highest level (non-political appointee) civil servant in one of the cabinet-level Departments of the Executive Branch of U.S. Government
- Manager of a drug/alcohol rehabilitation program
- Civil servant working in a large city government
- Manager of one of three world-wide offices of a major art gallery
- Chair of the Board of Education in a major city
- Coach of women's golf programs at two major NCAA universities

Board Members

- Board members of major airlines, financial institutions, and utilities in the United States
- Board members of major museums in the United States
- Board members of major hospitals in the United States

At first, I thought that summarizing the responses in some fashion would be the way to approach the responses from these leaders. However, I came to believe that just presenting their direct quotes (all or in part) made the most powerful statements about leadership. I have added my comments to some of the quotes, but my comments are minimal.

What follows are a number of the responses I received. I did a bit of editing as well. My comments are in italics. I believe just reading these direct quotes will give greater insight into the leadership roles than any summary.

Top Two or Three Leadership Qualities?

In the following section, I present a sample of the responses to the first question asked of the leaders:

- When you are in your leadership role, what are the two or three top qualities, things, capabilities, traits, etc. that you possess that make you an effective leader?

(And again, any comments I have are presented in italics.)

Skills and Abilities these Leaders Strongly Valued

A trait that I am always trying to build upon is **courage**—not being controlled by inner doubts, **being intellectually honest** and taking painful but critical risks to elevate my personal and team potential. *(Courage as part of the leader's make-up turned out to be a repeating thread in the responses.)*

Confidence: The ability to recognize your strengths and weaknesses.

Humility: Know the difference between leading and commanding. Using your own mind to make decisions that may be either against the trend or highly unpopular.

Compassion: Focus on outcomes, creativity.

Clear vision of what we want to achieve, strong communication skills, ability to recruit the right people for the right positions. *(Empowering, recruiting, and selecting the **right people** turned out to be a major theme in the responses.)*

Communication, confidence, commitment, and **knowing when to walk away**.

Excellent at finding the road to "Yes!"

Dependable, and always fair. **I treat everyone differently, but all are treated fairly.** *(I find this to be a very artful and thoughtful comment.)*

Listening to others' perspectives/fears/goals/capabilities; **helping them tailor their activities** in ways that are both aligned with organizational goals and consistent with their own perspectives/skills/needs.

I'm **able to articulate direction or strategy** in a way that makes it easier for people to understand and relate to. I'm able to understand their **particular personalities** and interact with them in a way that makes them feel they have the autonomy and desire to succeed.

Use of humor and encouragement of critical debate, with me being absolutely willing to stand down on decisions in the face of compelling arguments.

Hiring. Getting the right people is so key. Getting this wrong makes leading and managing more difficult. Set high expectations and standards. **People want to perform. They just need to know where to go.** Leading competent people often involved just staying out of the way.

Non-judgmental and promoting initiative (letting people learn from their mistakes, rather than punishing them for trying always yields pleasant returns.) Imperative for me to set the grand vision, set up the vast canvas and paint the broad strokes that lead to success. **Recruiting a GREAT team**, and give them the tools to succeed.

Ongoing philosophy of unconditional positive regard; people treated with respect and appreciation; **people working with me, *not* for me.**

Clarity of purpose. (I always wanted to be sure we understood the purpose of what we were doing and **how we were going to measure results.**)

Open and honest communication. (Whether upward, downward or sideways, it was important to me to be open and honest in sharing information and my opinions. Though it got me in some trouble, **people trusted me for this trait.**)

Treat people as colleagues. We were always in the game together. Same principle applied to my peers and higher ups. I cannot say I always found this easy, and would sometimes come to the conclusion that I did not trust or like someone. When the person worked for me, it was time for a change. I wish sometimes I had **cut the cord sooner** vs. giving the person another chance. If it was a boss, it was clearly **time for a change.**

Strategic and directional: try to see around corners and identify fault lines of change so we stay relevant to changing markets and clients without emasculating our soul and heritage.

Listen to and **embrace others' good ideas**, ideally to reinforce their contribution and encourage more from them.

Accountable: first, **admit my mistakes**; second, be responsive to and respectful of owners need for economic viability.

Being able to communicate and receive and understand communication is vital; how can one lead without such skill? A leader has to be able to exude confidence. That being said, confidence has perhaps a bigger role in the genesis of a leader and in its effectiveness. One has to believe in oneself to make decisions, to **avoid FEAR which usually leads to inaction.**

Impeccability, which is **doing one's best every time, whatever you are doing**, from sweeping the front door to dealing with an important client. Putting your best effort forward always pays off.

Leadership starts by building trust and confidence. In order to influence others and direct an organization, **you must be worthy of being followed.** I believe that building trust and confidence starts with honesty and integrity.

One leader offered these three points:

1. Honesty and **authenticity** are critical.

2. Courage and confidence. By the time one is a leader, that person will have acquired much of the necessary "technical skills." What is required is the confidence in oneself and **the courage to act.**

3.   The **willingness to know yourself**. This is an ongoing process and a struggle. It allows one to accept challenges and differing points of view as well as to accept and deal with one's own weaknesses.

And a different person presented these ideas:

1.   Don't ask anyone to do something you would not do yourself.

2.   There's only one team...and only the team wins.

3.   Think strategically but act tactically.

Finally, some additional comments from other leaders:

Preparation: This means spending an inordinate amount of time researching, drafting documents, and outlining goals. Listening to the team input is very crucial to preparation. **Participation:** I believe critical tasks are a shared responsibility. **Perseverance**: Keep goals in mind and complete them. Focus on task with all team members.

Setting the direction of the organization, keeping the mission/reason for being in front of all constituents, Board, customers, employees. Keeping focus: You manage what you measure; you have to know whether you're winning or losing: 3-5 goals or objectives are all that anyone can handle.

An appropriate sense of urgency. Organizations need that edge. Employees need a sense of urgency.

So, as you can see, quite a variety of responses from these leaders, some similar, and some unique and singular in nature. Having read through their responses, did you see any surprises?

Areas Where the Leaders Wanted to Improve

Now, let us move on to an examination of what skills these leaders said they wanted to develop or expand upon. Once again, this second question was:

- What is one quality, capability, trait, etc,. that you would like to improve upon in your role as a leader?

Presented below is a sample of the responses to the question. Each bullet point represents the response of a single individual. To keep your focus, I am slightly altering my style in presenting the responses to this second question. Also, I've informally sorted them into some general categories that emerged as I looked at the responses:

Improve Communication Goal

- Quality, **timeliness of feedback**—both positive and negative

- I'd like to **be more verbose** in my communication style—it's too terse

- Communication of **vision**

- Be more **direct**

- I would like to communicate more effectively, and tone **down the emotions**

- **Communicating to the organization**. (I believe that most leaders underestimate the importance of communication. This should be a daily agenda item, not an afterthought. We can get complacent and assume that everyone is on the same page.)

- **My use of constructive criticism**. It's challenging to look back without inferring mistakes and oversights. Looking in the mirror at my own errors has been equally crucial

Address Conflict Goal

- I would like to be **better at confronting people with difficult issues** or take difficult actions. (Effectively confronting or challenging others was an area that many respondents found particularly difficult)

- Conflict management/resolution

- Thing I should **not have done is be too soft**. I should not have been a "Heidi," but it has not come back to bite me that often. I should have learned not to bring the work home with me. That hurts the ones you love

Have a Better Focus Goal

- Ability to concentrate on issues for a longer time

- **I get bored too easily** which can lead to lack of operational follow though and whimsical changes in tactics

- **Over-scheduling,** and being able to say no and not feel I am letting someone down

- **Working on the highest priority items first** rather than those that are easy. (I think this is an important comment--an easy trap to fall in. I think we all need to ask ourselves if we do this, and can it be a problem for us.)

Develop Followership Goal

- **I didn't do the trust-building** when it counted most for the organization and the mission of the organization

- My ability to inspire others into action; **making others feel they are fully vested in and part of a process**, and helping them understand and believe that their opinion and input matter

- Engaging others as volunteers in taking on long-range stewardship of projects

- I need to **be more empathetic**, more understanding of limitations of others

- Improve my **ability to motivate others to action**. (And what follows is a comment by this respondent that is very personal. Perhaps others in leadership positions also may believe this about themselves but never articulate it):

Truthfully, I don't much enjoy the "leadership" role, and **am much more comfortable and effective as #2, supporting a #1** who has the ego-drive and motivational skills that I lack

Improve Administrative and Technical Skills Goal

- Create schedules; use a bit **more structure**

- More **data driven**, less intuition

- Delegate tasks

- **Delegation of authority** (Somewhat surprising to me, delegation of authority also frequently emerged as a trait to be improved upon).

More Self-Knowledge Goal

- More self-awareness

- Not selling myself short; consistently showing conviction

- Looking back **there were times I was too hasty in making a decision**. Being decisive also worked in a positive way many times. However it is an area where I could have improved my judgment regarding when to act more carefully.

- Because the last four years have been so intense and demanding, and I had to focus on the right now and near future, I don't look back often enough to what has brought **happiness, friendship, connection and strength**. Being able to maintain a **balance in my life-mental/physical/emotional**--has become critical.

Hopefully, a response or two from the above two sections touched a nerve for you and may help you in your leadership role. And though there were many unique comments on the leadership subject, there were also common themes stated in different ways that may be useful to you.

My personal thanks to everyone who looked at their personal leadership styles and talked about what they thought they did best and where they might improve. I believe these insights will be useful in charting your leadership development path.

Manage *Your* Career: No One Else Will

One aspect of being a leader that I believe does not get enough emphasis is the ongoing process of the leader proactively managing his or her career. This has been a very important aspect of my career, and in the sections below, I offer some of my thoughts regarding career management.

Networking: Making Yourself Effective in the World

One key skill that next generation leaders (and certainly current leaders!) need to have is the ability to manage one's own career. Most of us don't do this very well, as we get wrapped up in our work and do not periodically take time to pause, reflect, and consider our future direction.

In the section below, I present a model that I have found very helpful in managing my own career. And over the years, I have shared this model with others, who have likewise found it to be helpful. And re-emphasizing a prior point that bears repeating, just because this approach may make sense does not make it easy.

I formally utilized this approach in the "outplacement" world, where people who had lost their jobs came to me for help in finding new positions.

Intuitive, But Difficult to Apply

I think the approach and the specific steps to take within this approach are almost intuitive and just about everyone should not only be able to understand them, but should also be able to integrate and apply them immediately. Not so.

Many times, people nod in agreement when I present the details of my model (reflecting its intuitive nature). However, they frequently do not follow through on its implementation. Again, human nature.

This is hard work. Generally, people like to look for the easy option available to them rather than the hard one. So don't be surprised if you tend to pick "easy" over "hard," even though *easy* may not be very productive.

Please keep these comments in mind as you read the details presented in the following sections. Additionally, when reading these various career management processes, look for those situations where *you*, too, may be tempted to choose "easy" over "hard."

But How Will I Know Whom to Contact?

Now, how do you get the names of the people you should contact? I suggest that you write down the names of every person you know, and I mean everyone, including relatives.

Each person you contact has their own view and take on the world and will have a unique viewpoint on what they think you should do, even if they've known you for years. This includes mother, father, brothers, sisters, best friends, co-workers, social contacts, people you haven't had contact with in years, people who you may not have hit it off with all that well but still might accept a contact from you.

Write every name down. (And when I've counseled in this area, I always suggest people that my clients never thought of, like barbers, hairdressers, bartenders, friends of siblings who you also know, etc.).

Write Down *All* the Names that Come to Mind

As I mentioned, write down everyone that comes to mind. Then, I suggest you divide the names into three categories and put the number 1, 2 or 3 beside each name. The first category would be those people with whom you feel comfortable. In other words, they know you and will forgive faults you present when you meet with them.

The second category would be those people you want to meet with when you have everything together—confident in presenting yourself, etc.

The third category would be those people who you do not think would immediately be able to assist you—but in this category, "you never know." These are people with whom you can test and try things out—you may feel you have nothing to lose by meeting with them.

As an example, I once had a client whose wife participated in a garden club. She spoke with the head of her garden club, whose husband was Chief Executive Officer of a company. Through the head of the garden club, the wife arranged a meeting for her husband with the CEO. The husband ended up being hired. So, my point is that no matter how unlikely a contact might seem, you never know unless you try.

Be Able to *Briefly* Summarize Who You Are

This step is known as the "elevator speech." If you were at the top floor of an elevator and had to explain who you are to someone before reaching the bottom floor, could you do it? It sounds easy, but it's not.

For me, this description has three parts:

1. A brief history of who you are, obviously focusing on a few key high points

2. Being able to describe what you are hoping to accomplish and do next

3. What makes you unique? (This is perhaps the most important part)

Remember, this short "speech" needs to have a purpose. You want to elicit enough interest that the person wants to stay engaged with you and help you achieve your goal.

Get "Adopted"

We've all had the situation when a brief conversation or interview went on much, much longer than anticipated. This is the initial step in having the other person do what I call "adopting you."

For you to get "adopted," the other person has to develop enough interest in you to want to continue engaging with you. It's a nice feeling, isn't it?

When this "adoption" seems to be happening, I suggest using a question or variation of this question to move the conversation in the direction you want. And this question is open ended. In other words, the person chooses where to take his or her answer with no direction from you. An example of such a question is:

- "If you were in my shoes, what would you do? Where would you look? Who would you talk to?"

Another way of phrasing this question is:

- "If you were me, what would you do next?"

People like to be asked for their opinion and advice. An indication that you are moving toward "adoption" is if the other person is doing most of the talking. If you are doing all the talking in the conversation, you aren't likely at the adoption stage. This means you need to be careful about interrupting and trying to present every strength of yours.

This is hard. You are likely in a pressured situation where you want to make sure the person has full knowledge of the wonderful person you are. So it's sometimes very hard for you to just calmly and attentively listen to the advice you are being given. Of course this is a balancing act, but the key is for you not to dominate the conversation, especially if you have the opportunity to do so.

The open-ended question might get you an unexpected and helpful response. That open-ended question might also get you a response that is so far off base that you need to re-direct the conversation. You are always thankful for any advice you receive, no matter how off-base it might be. If you communicate that the advice is *not* good, it may shut down the other person, and then you would not receive perhaps the next bit of advice or suggestion that could be quite useful to you.

Again, this is hard. It's always easy to say what's on your mind, for example: "Oh, I already thought of that and tried it, and it didn't work out for me." Gratefully accept all information and sort it out later. You don't need to follow up on anything. You *do* need to show appreciation so the person continues to suggest what he or she would do if they were you.

But again, sometimes the open-ended advice does not make any sense. You then need to shift the direction of the person's response by asking close-ended type questions. These may be more specific and often can be answered with a yes/no answer. Examples of questions directing the conversation to a specific area are:

- "Do you know anyone at Xyz company?" or
- "Do you know anyone in the marketing field?"

When you get specific answers to these types of close-ended questions, you can then switch back and forth between the types of questions to get more information, like "How do you think I could best contact the person at Xyz Company?"

Can You Get a "Warm" Introduction?

The very best way to meet the people whose names you've been given is if the person making the referral actually contacted the person on your behalf to set up a meeting.

By doing so, you automatically receive a very strong positive reference. However, people who give you names, especially if you've just met them, are not likely to contact their referrals on your behalf. In such a situation, you should ask something like the following:

- "Thank you for this referral. If it's OK with you, when I call or email to set up an appointment, I'd like to use your name."

Make sure to get the referrer's agreement. You then have a reference, though not as powerful as the direct contact.

Now we're entering the hardest part of this process. Remember this obvious but painful reality:

- People don't wake up in the morning thinking they'd like to meet with you.

So, often when you contact a person you've been referred to, they are not anxious to meet with you and many will not, no matter what steps you go through. It's always hard to handle rejection, and when people decline your invitation for a meeting, it feels like a strong rejection.

But it's important not to take this rejection personally and move on to your next attempt at networking. Here is a short, self-talk phrase that can help you during the slow periods of networking:

- "People who decline to meet with me do not yet know me."

Face-to Face Meetings: Optimal

I cannot emphasize enough the importance of face-to-face meetings. Why?

It's hard to be adopted over the phone or through an email. People will not be willing to work on your behalf if there is not a personal connection. So, the name of the game is getting face-to-face with those with whom you are trying to connect.

Although I emphasize the importance of face-to-face meetings, sometimes they are not possible for a variety of reasons. In such situations, telephone referrals are much better than email referrals. If you do get an email referral, in your email to the contact, after giving a bit of a written 'elevator' speech, ask when a good time to call them might be as well as convenient times for such a call. Keep gently pushing for the type of contact that will present you in the best possible light.

What *Do* You Say To Them?

Particularly with people you are meeting for the first time, ask for a brief meeting (10 to 15 minutes). People consider their time valuable, and in many cases it is!

In those 10 or 15 minutes, you will give your elevator speech and ask good questions. If the meeting goes longer than the time you asked for, you know you're in the process of being adopted. This has happened to all of us at various points during the course of our lives.

And out of each meeting, you should ask for at least two referrals. Ask something like:

- "Might you suggest two or three people you think I should contact?"

Again, when given the names, ask if you can use the referrer's name when you contact the new individuals. You might also ask the referrer for their advice on the best way to make the contact.

It's a Numbers Game

And here's where it gets really tough.

If you're searching for employment, the process is a numbers game. The more people you contact, the higher your odds of a successful interview. But, each rejection can make it harder to place the next call or write the next email attempting to get a meeting. Yet, you still have to do it. When you are involved in this process, it's important to set a goal each day for the number of contacts you will make. Then you have at least one way of measuring your effort.

How Will *You* Manage *Your* Time?

So much of this process involves time management. I do not suggest spending an inordinate amount of time following up on long-shot opportunities. It's important to focus on those efforts that you feel will most likely pay off. Having said this, I'd carve out a little time to follow up with some people in the long-shot group. This category is a relatively safe opportunity for you plus it lets you practice and become comfortable in the interviewing process.

Also, permit yourself to follow up with "dream" positions. Think: "If I could have any position, what would it be?" Regardless of your qualifications for such a position, giving yourself permission to spend a little of your time following up in this area can be exciting and rejuvenating for you.

Keep the Faith: It Takes Time

As I said before, one of the most difficult things to do is to keep at this process, particularly when results are not immediate. And as difficult as this process is, particularly if you are feeling internal pressures, it can also be a very positive experience. Because of the wide range of people and situations you'll be led to by following these steps, you will find yourself talking with and considering opportunities you never imagined.

Though much of the process is difficult, parts of the process are fun. And back to an earlier key point: if you can realistically think of the positive aspects of this process, you will behave in a positive manner with those you meet. Behaving positively gives you a greater chance of the person being willing to put him or herself in your position and make recommendations on how you should move forward.

If I Could Do It All Over Again...

This section is a collection of recent reflections I've had regarding my career, my priorities, and what I would do differently if I were to have the proverbial second chance.

When I was in my 40s, I thought about my career up to that point, and came to a conclusion. I had been quite successful in my mid-30s, culminating with a senior position at a major bank. But there was a price to pay. If I am honest, my first priority was my work, and family responsibilities were a distant second.

My social life mostly encompassed activities drawn from the business side of life. If I were to have a second chance at my life, I would do this part over and focus more on my family and not on business.

Carl Jung (2006), the famous psychotherapist, once said something like the first half of a man's life is accomplishing things outside of himself; the second half is focusing on his internal life. My focus was not balanced between home, family and business but far over-weighted to the business side of life.

Along the lines of the Jung comment, I viewed my life in my 40s as having entered into a second chapter. In retrospect, I had viewed my first half as "climbing" the corporate ladder (and though I think this type of time allocation was more common with men of my generation, it's my sense that perhaps women and men are returning to this imbalance in today's corporate world, especially in the technology arena).

Leaving My 40s: Breadth of Work Focus *and* Personal Development

Starting in my 40s I began looking across my business career, seeking experiences that not only expanded my business experiences, but also expanded my personal development as well. This meant more of a focus on what was meaningful to me in my life, with business still playing an important but only a partial part of my life.

In this second half, I have placed my emphasis on "broadening," in both my corporate and personal worlds.

I spent some of this decade having a focus on clinical counseling, as evidenced by my time working as a clinician in a community based drug and alcohol program focusing on clients within both the criminal justice system and the Child Protective Services world. This experience brought strong new perspectives into my awareness, and fueled the creation of a different perspective when I later returned to a position in the corporate world.

My 50s: Corporate Re-Entry with a Different Mindset

During my late 50s, I re-entered the corporate world.

I was one of the oldest employees in this technology company, given the standard focus on youth within the world of technology. I consciously chose to do things differently in the corporation at this stage of my life.

- Rather than have my focus be upward, I determined that my primary focus would be to develop those within my department and place my emphasis laterally across the organization.

My new approach of focusing across and downward turned out to be a major source of satisfaction during this stage of my career. Somehow, I'd arrived at an understanding of what was important in my personal life and my business life and I was able to manage a relatively healthy balance between the two, which I think worked to the betterment of both.

As Time Goes By, Minimize Your "Groveling"

We have all been in situations where we sacrificed a bit of our soul in service of reaching a goal. We may have tried too hard to impress, or minimized our values in order to achieve something important, possibly during a time of fear or need. Or, maybe we let our need for approval (or other needs of the ego) get the best of us, acting in ways that weren't really us.

For me, these situations constitute the process of "groveling." Now, some sources claim the word "grovel" is an Old Norse term, relating to operating "on one's belly."

Other sources illustrate groveling with the following:

- Treating someone with too much respect in a way that suggests my weakness—or desperation—in order to gain approval or favor
- Behaving in an awkwardly humble manner, or with artificial humility, as if facing a higher authority

Though the word *groveling* is used by me in a somewhat tongue-in-cheek manner, there definitely is an element of truth in its use in a business setting.

One of the things I'm most thankful for in my semi-retired state from the business world is that I no longer feel the need to "grovel."

In looking back at my career, given my personality, I see many occasions where internal panic set in and I would go to what I even then considered extremes to accomplish what I felt was needed. Shakespeare's quote, "To thine own self be true," was not always operative when I was in a sales mode, or when I was looking for a job.

For me the word *groveling* had its strongest impact when I was in a sales mode. Though I've always presented myself fairly well, I never felt comfortable "selling," even when that was my job. So I often found myself going beyond where I would normally go, mostly in the vain hope of "making the sale." I wasn't proud of my behavior, but somehow I felt the internal pressure to continue on this path, even though I should have stopped long before. Actually, I felt ashamed of my behavior, but still kept at it.

In the workplace, I believe we all have to go beyond our comfort zones and behave in a manner we might not always be totally comfortable with. But I also think it's useful to be aware of feelings we are repressing when we do so.

You may be aware of similar reactions to some of your behaviors. When I have faced problematic situations, I've found it is helpful to 'label' that behavior. If you are aware you just 'groveled' and are not pleased with it, by telling yourself (or others) that you did so often takes the internal sting out of such behavior.

After I became conscious of my groveling behavior, and called myself on it, I found I would chuckle at myself. The behavior did not have the heavy, ponderous reaction it once did before I laughed at myself.

- So, my encouragement to you is to be aware of those situations or settings where you are most at risk to grovel, and make appropriate, conscious adjustments in your behavior as you see best.

Concluding Thoughts

Offering concluding thoughts on the broad topic of leadership is very challenging. So, true to the goal of this chapter, which has been to present my experiential-based views on leadership, I have saved some special responses from two of the leaders in my survey.

These responses, I believe, represent both sophisticated and highly personal, humanistic approaches to being a leader. Here are some responses from the first of these two individuals:

- "My father once told me that it seemed like a waste of a life for someone to live their life and not leave the world a better place than they found it."

- "I never met her, but many years ago I read and will always remember (the recently deceased) Maya Angelou's comment that people will forget what you did, but they will never forget how you made them feel."

And, this person adds:

- "The guy I bought my first company from told me to not worry about what the other guy is getting but to focus on whether I am getting what is enough for me."

Now, presented below are some very powerful comments from one of the surveyed leaders. Who is this person?

Well, the best way for me to introduce them to you is to tell you that I often refer to this person as "the best leader I worked for." Here are snippets of this person's survey responses; you'll quickly see why I describe them as the best leader for whom I've worked:

- "A leader needs to believe in the goal. This belief can be about the need and superiority of a product, or the approach of the company or anything that makes the leader passionate to pursue this path. Without passion, leadership doesn't matter. A leader requires others to accept these goals and follow. A leader has to make their passion infectious. They have to spread it wide. They have to have others adopt it as their own in order to achieve it. Hence, the ability to translate the vision into action requires communication."

And now a second response from this leader:

- "Communication is not necessarily about superior oratory skills. It is about sincere sharing, in a simple synopsis, why the leader needs you. A leader has to communicate constantly at many levels. I believe leaders must be examples, they must partake in the efforts, shoulder to shoulder with the rest. Inspiration is the greatest tool available to a leader. And to inspire, you have to lead from the front."

Finally, when this leader responded to the question of what they should improve upon, here is what they said:

- "I need to be more empathetic, more enabling, more understanding of limitations of others. I realize that every person would like to be a high performer. When they can't, it is because of hurdles they feel impaired by. As a leader, we typically sideline poor performers, we diminish them, we reject them. We often feel no remorse to the harm we have caused to the soul of this person. To leave a person with hope and potential of their possibilities even when I have no need for them in my path is something I want to strive for. No person I come in touch with should be marked negatively by their interaction with me. If I cannot inspire them, I at least should not be the cause of their poor performance."

Powerful thoughts and goals, from a leader with global success. We should all strive to live by such leadership tenets.

Chapter 11
The Gift of Positive Psychology: Fuel for Future Leaders

Jonathan R. Flannes

Jonathan Flannes works as a behavioral modification coach for a large non-profit mental health agency which provides mental health, school, community-based, and family treatment services for high-risk children and their families. In his role, he offers behavioral support techniques to such youth and their families. He sees the application of positive psychology techniques as a valuable resource for such children and their families. However, in this chapter, he takes his interest in positive psychology and describes how he thinks effective leaders need to have a positive psychology "practice" in their lives in order to achieve their own high levels of performance while also creating success-oriented work cultures for their employees. He believes that the development of positive psychology personal attributes can be a developmental focus for leaders of all ages—and especially for next generation leaders, who, like himself, represent that group of millennials who have recently entered the workforce. He may be reached at jonathanflannes@gmail.com.

I am early in my career, and I represent the "next generation" in the title of this book, those of us in our 20s and 30s. I believe that those of us in this generation will discover benefits in applying the ideas of positive psychology as we begin to engage in roles as leaders.

In this chapter, I apply the concepts of positive psychology to a variety of environments wherein I have worked, noting what "positive psychology qualities" were held by the leaders I have respected in each of these settings. These work settings include an inner-city youth program, the world of performing arts, and a top-end advertising and communications firm.

What Makes For a Good Leader?

Determining what makes a good leader is a difficult task. Some people may say that good leadership is situation-specific, while others might argue that there are attributes of good leadership that transcend setting or context. In this chapter, I will use my work experiences from the above-mentioned job settings as the basis for supporting the following idea:

- Good leaders, regardless of job title or industry, hold many personal attributes consistent with the core tenets of positive psychology

In this chapter, I focus specifically on the positive psychology contributions of Martin Seligman, Ph.D., and Mihaly Csikszentmihalyi, Ph.D. These renowned proponents of positive psychology have spoken extensively on the need to develop a branch of psychology that examines those aspects of human behavior/experience that best contribute to lives being lead at optimal levels of functioning (Seligman and Csikszentmihalyi, 2000). Such an approach differs from many traditional approaches to psychology, whose primary focus is often one of diagnosing conditions and/or reducing dysfunctional behaviors or emotions. The application of positive psychology continues to grow, as evidenced by recent reviews and publications (Donaldson, Dollwet, and Rao, 2014).

My First Reaction to Positive Psychology: Guarded

My first exposure to the concepts of positive psychology took place as student at New York University, where I obtained my degree in Applied Psychology. In fulfilling the degree's requirements, I took a course entitled "The Science of Happiness," and, for obvious reasons, it filled up quickly.

While I tried to enter the class with an open mind, I have to say, my initial reaction was one of doubt and tentative disapproval. From the outset, I imagined positive psychology to be an endless promotion of "looking on the bright side" and "forgetting the past," while minimizing the psychological importance of addressing issues like trauma or abuse, mood disorders, and grief.

However, as the course progressed, I was surprised and pleased to be exposed to a collection of unique theories and ideas often absent in one's traditional psychology education. Instead of focusing primarily on dysfunction and/or relief from psychological issues (which can be emphasized in a problem-reduction focused psychology), positive psychology took a different path. This path focused on approaches that one could follow in hope of experiencing personal happiness and satisfaction, the ability to thrive during difficult times, and the chance to pursue one's full potential. By the end of the course, I was hooked, excited by the *sense of possibility* demonstrated in all of the positive psychology models we explored.

Additionally, as the course moved towards completion, I also started to see the possible application of positive psychology to roles of leadership. I reflected back upon my previous work experiences, and I noticed the best leaders for whom I worked, regardless of the industry, held many attributes consistent with core principles of positive psychology.

- Soon, I was beginning to see that positive psychology is not just a way of *living*, it's also a way of *leading.*

What Is Positive Psychology?

Only through an understanding of the basic conceptual underpinnings of positive psychology can we explore its value in the world of leadership. From what I have found, I view positive psychology as an examination of the attitudes, attributes, and behaviors that promote optimal levels of human potential and performance.

A more formal definition of positive psychology comes from the Positive Psychology Center (www.ppc.sas.upenn.edu) of the University of Pennsylvania, where Dr. Seligman is currently involved. In the words of the Center, positive psychology can be defined as:

> the scientific study of the strengths and virtues that enable individuals and communities to thrive. The field is founded on the belief that people want

to lead meaningful and fulfilling lives, to cultivate what is best within themselves, and to enhance their experiences of love, work, and play.

As I mentioned earlier, I will confine my application of positive psychology approaches to Seligman and his PERMA model, and Csikszentmihalyi and his view of *flow* activities.

What is PERMA?

Dr. Seligman (2012) has crafted a positive psychology model that I believe leaders of all capacities should consider. This model is termed PERMA, and consists of the following (in my words) building blocks of well-being:

P: The presence of *positive emotions*, a sense of feeling good, accepting that life has its normal ups and downs

E: Being *engaged* in the world and in your activities. For me, this sounds like another way of thinking about the ability to be present, not living in the past or the future

R: Being in *relationship* with others, feeling a sense of connectedness with your associates

M: Having *meaning* in your life, a sense that your existence matters, and that you are pursuing tasks that give you a sense of value or purpose

A: *Achieving* in life, completing tasks or projects that give you the experience of accomplishment or success.

I believe that good, effective leaders have many of Seligman's PERMA qualities. If you take a close look at the PERMA list, I believe you will see a very clear emphasis on one getting him- or herself "together," and I believe this goal to be an important first step for any effective leader. As evidence of the importance of this and similar models, consider this fact: Dr. Seligman's model of positive psychology has been applied to leadership and personal functioning in a number of significant areas, including, among others, the United States Army (Reivich, Seligman, and McBride, 2011).

Csikszentmihalyi and *Flow*

The powerful concepts of flow and flow activities have been articulated by Mihaly Csikszentmihalyi (Csikszentmihalyi and Csikszentmihalyi, 1992). His work addresses the flow experience in a variety of settings, often describing the powerful experiences present when one is immersed in an artistic processes. However, it is his discussion on the impact of flow upon leadership that I find to be most valuable. His work on flow has served as a core element of the Positive Psychology Program at Claremont Graduate University in California.

Flow (introduced in Chapter 6) involves one's engagement in an activity in which the individual experiences effortless immersion, intense focus, energetic pursuit, true enjoyment, and diminished levels of self-consciousness and time tracking. When one completes a flow activity, that person often feels emotionally and intellectually refreshed. I know that is how I feel when I complete one of my flow activities.

For example, some of my own flow activities include: writing and performing music (both instrumental and vocal), immersion in meaningful conversations, active engagement in an outdoor activity, and studying almost anything related to European history. Following my involvement in such flow activities, I find that I feel more alive, optimistic, and less prone to worrying about situations out of my control.

In the following section, I will present leaders I have worked for whom I respected, and whom I felt were very effective. I will offer my thoughts on how these individuals exhibited qualities consistent with the PERMA model attributes. Additionally, I will describe activities engaged in by these leaders that I view as constituting their own flow activities.

My Work Settings

As mentioned at the beginning of the chapter, I have held positions in a number of different industries. I have selected three jobs from which I gather my observations on what I perceive as effective leadership, and I try to make the connection to their PERMA attributes and their involvement with their own flow activities. These work settings include:

- A non-profit center for at-risk youth

- The performing arts

- A top-end advertising and communications firm

Observations on Leaders: Examples of PERMA and Flow in My Work Settings

The first work setting I will cover is the area of social services, looking specifically at an urban youth program where I worked.

Inner-City Youth Program

Description: This clinic provided a breadth of social, educational, and psychological support services for "high-risk" youth, many of whom were victims of abuse or neglect, or were lacking the resources/opportunities to forge a promising future.

My job: The position I held was one of an intake counselor, meeting with new clients to document and assess their basic psychological history, while simultaneously watching for signs of drug use, abuse, and/or suicidality. Following my intake assessment with a new client, I would share with him or her the resources we offered, directing them to the departments most beneficial, given their current needs.

One leader's special qualities/behaviors: I found one leader at the organization to be particularly impressive. She possessed a boundless energy. This energy and enthusiasm proved to be highly contagious, encouraging our adoption of this important trait in the highly fast-paced environment in which we operated. Over time, it became clear that her enthusiasm was motivated by a powerful *sincerity of purpose* directed at helping the diverse group of teens in need of our services. Her work was not just a *job*, it was a *calling*. Reflecting upon my time at this organization, I view this leader's strong sense of commitment and purpose as representative of:

- The *Meaning* and *Achieving* components of Seligman's PERMA model

Additionally, our leader, when speaking with my fellow counselors and me, possessed a keen ability to relate to us as though we were the only people in the world. In conversation, she often promoted an atmosphere of free-form communication among the staff, and we benefited greatly from her desire to facilitate the developmental needs of all of us. By holding regular, interactive staff meetings designed for us to share our experiences of the organization (both the good and the bad), she created an open, non-judgmental work environment. This practice proved to be one of the most important aspects of her leadership, providing us with a feeling of comfort when we were discussing the various obstacles we encountered in our work.

The qualities detailed above reflect this leader's ability to operate within:

- Seligman's *Presence* and *Engagement* attributes from the PERMA model

Cumulatively, the leader's application of these PERMA qualities, assisted me, as a staff member, in:

- Feeling excited and motivated, knowing our leader was giving it her all

- Having a sense of comfort, knowing that mistakes would be *explored* rather than *criticized*

- Holding a sincere belief in the organization's mission

The World of Performing Arts

Description: During another period in my life, I was a founding member of an independent musical band, serving as songwriter, vocalist, and guitarist. We played and recorded together for a number of years, performing at venues (both large and small) across the United States.

My role: Songwriter, vocalist, guitarist

One leader's special qualities/behaviors: The leader I wish to describe in this setting served as both *manager* and *mentor*, a very challenging leadership combination to implement.

Perhaps the most admirable of his leadership traits was the strong sense of *meaning and purpose* he possessed. Having worked with artists, both large and small, successful and struggling, he believed that his professional goal was to help up-and-coming groups receive proper attention and promotion. With this solid sense of purpose and meaning, he devoted his attention to promoting acts like us, resulting in a level of success we had never imagined (including national tours, record sales, and major label attention). He would later go on to utilize his sense of purpose to do the same with numerous other acts, some now performing on the world stage.

However, what served us the most was his exceptional ability to form and nurture positive relationships. As one can imagine, to function properly, the music industry relies upon a complex web of relationships, often in constant communication. In such a cutthroat business, we were surprised to find ourselves gaining ground at a rapid pace, and soon realized the incredible value his relationships possessed. Whether the conversations were with promoters, record labels, or within the group itself, we always trusted that such positive interpersonal connections would move us forward.

The qualities detailed above reflect this leader's ability to operate within:

- Seligman's *Positive Relationships* and *Meaning* from the PERMA model

The leader's application of these PERMA qualities assisted me, as a band member, in working:

- Towards continual progress in solidifying business relationships

- With a sense that what we were doing *mattered*

- To actively communicate with my peers, especially in times of disagreement

To shift the focus to me, I found that I functioned at my interpersonal best in this work setting when I was actively seeking out time for my own flow experiences. By engaging in my own flow activities (such as individually working on my own music creations), I discovered that I:

- Could keep a sharp focus on tasks when my leadership skills were required

- Had a greater ability to bounce back and be my best in the face of the physically and emotionally demanding aspects of touring and performing

Advertising & Communications Agency

Description: Corporate advertising

My role: Market researcher

One leader's special qualities/behaviors: Our team leader held a number of desirable traits that resulted in increased productivity and employee morale.

Specifically, this leader practiced a wide variety of *flow activities*, including a combination of hobbies and regular exercise to provide her with a balanced and fulfilling life. It appeared to me that this balance gave her a foundation for being an inspiring and energizing leader, even during the most challenging work periods.

Her modeling her involvement with her flow activities created a healthy and refreshing presence in the office. We were all very grateful to have a leader whose positive emotional compass served as a voice of comfort throughout difficult times.

She was professional yet approachable, business-minded yet empathetic. Unlike many of her colleagues, she was far from being a "workaholic," and chose to spend her time in a balanced, meaningful manner (with her flow activities). Along with the hobbies she pursued outside of work, she maintained a consistent devotion to her family and friends, regardless of how hectic her work life became. This harmonious approach to life left her refreshed and *present,* leading the team with the focus and encouragement.

Additionally, her pursuit of *accomplishment* also proved to be valuable in lifting her spirits. As department leader, her hard work had paid off, and the joy she gathered from this success rubbed off onto her fellow employees.

It's my contention that the qualities detailed above reflect this leader's ability to operate with:

- Csikszentmihalyi's application of *flow* as a regenerative process

- Seligman's *Accomplishment* from the PERMA model

Personally, I found that the leader's application of these flow and PERMA qualities assisted me, as a staff member, in:

- Reminding myself to stay invested with my own flow activities

- Feeling better equipped in addressing our leaders and clients in a more confident manner, as I could witness that each small accomplishment of mine increased my sense of value and contribution

In Table 11.1, I present a brief overview of the positive psychology behaviors I have noticed with the three leaders I have been describing.

Table 11.1

Work Setting Examples of Positive Psychology-Based Leadership Behavior

Work Setting	Positive Leadership Behavior Observed	Indicative of Positive Psychology (PERMA or Flow)
Inner-city youth program	Presence Engagement	PERMA
Performing arts group	Positive Relationships Meaning	PERMA
Advertising agency	Personal activities of meaning Accomplishment	Flow PERMA

Positive Psychology and Its Impact on Me

Because my initial impression of positive psychology was one of doubt and disinterest, I never would have imagined the integral part it would play in triggering substantial emotional and personal growth for me. I've noticed that since I have become involved in the world of positive psychology, I've gratefully developed the following:

1. A more steady sense of optimism, being more cognizant of the variety of qualities and activities (PERMA and Flow) that play a huge part in supporting my happiness

2. An awareness that all periods, good and bad, will pass

3. The motivation to continue to utilize music and the arts (some of my own flow activities) as sources for my own peace and contentment

4. A strengthening of my desire to make the world a better place

5. The ability to function more often at the *top of my game* through a clarity of communication, confidence, and willingness to engage in challenging leadership tasks

Including Positive Psychology in Your life

One other positive psychology-based intervention warrants comment, as it is a simple but powerful tool, and I believe it can have an immediate, positive impact on your life.

I am referring here to the general practice of applying *gratitude*, and the specific practice of keeping a gratitude journal.

Simply put, keeping a gratitude journal can be no more involved than briefly writing down one thing at the end of your day for which you feel gratitude. Your entries in your daily gratitude journal, which only need to take a few minutes of your time, may represent "small things," as well as "big things."

A listing of the small things for which you may feel gratitude, for example, could include feeling grateful that:

- Your bus came on time today

- The sun finally emerged from the rain clouds

- Your day ended earlier than you first thought it would

Examples of "big things" for which you may feel gratitude at the end of any one day could include:

- The fact that your family members all returned home safely that night

- You finally started feeling stronger after a long struggle back from pneumonia

- Your aunt did not receive another round of frightening medical news during her recent hospitalization

Personally, by using my own gratitude journal, I have found that I:

- Can more easily focus on what I do have in my life, as compared to what I don't have

- Am able to maintain greater perspective on issues that trouble me

- Feel more energy, and experience greater productivity

- Hold greater empathy for others

Obviously, when I project myself into new leadership roles, I see that I will want to use my gratitude journal as a key positive psychology tool for assisting me in being the best leader I can be.

Future Leadership Applications

As technology continues to advance and change the world in which we live, I believe future leaders will increasingly want to turn to the application of positive psychology for both personal and professional growth. This may be the case for leaders in a plethora of different settings, from small businesses to government, education to foreign policy. A handful of examples come to mind in which leaders could utilize positive psychology to the betterment of society. They include:

- Practicing healthy, beneficial flow activities in our over-stimulated, distraction-oriented world (i.e., endless YouTube, Facebook, Twitter, etc.)

- The development of optimism for political leaders functioning in areas of great instability and violence (i.e., the Middle East, and Eastern Europe)

- Creating a culture of empathy towards those in need (i.e., the economically disadvantaged, the mentally ill, and the drug addicted)

As I mentioned previously, I view positive psychology as *a way of leading*, and *not just a way of living*. I have found positive psychology approaches to be tangible and practical. I encourage all leaders, from those currently in leadership roles to those next-generation leaders who have not yet formally assumed such leadership roles, to actively embrace positive psychology. It will benefit you by helping you be the best you can be, and by implication, that will help your team members do the same.

Chapter 12
Leadership: What Can Your Future Hold?

Steven Flannes

Enterprise challenges in the future will require that you continue to develop your psychological and interpersonal nimbleness; that is, your ability to size up an interpersonal situation, and then promptly identify the appropriate, interpersonally sophisticated response for the situation will be crucial.

You will need flexibility in the way you process your own emotional reactions. Less and less will you be able to encounter an interpersonal leadership problem, and then "think about it" or retreat to your office to consider your best response.

Speed of working, and the pace of interpersonal transactions, will require that you bring "mindfulness" to each interpersonal interaction. Being mindful (see Chapter 9) means you do not want to be carrying the weight of unprocessed emotional baggage from previous events. Such an idea implies that you can use resilience (Chapter 6) in helping you bounce back from demanding situations.

Your mindfulness (which at its core suggests that you bring an intellectual and emotional openness to each interaction) will increase your ability to be "present" when relating to your stakeholders. By being present, you will:

- Communicate your interest in hearing what the other person is saying

- Present an image of you, the leader, as someone who can intently grasp the message and needs of others

- Be able to process more information and data from the people for whom this should be your priority—your team members, related stakeholders, and your customers

I believe your ability to be present is your most important leadership attribute. The technical stuff you can learn as needed. However, if you are not able to be present, you will be hampered in leading and influencing others. And after all, isn't project management really, at the end of the day, getting work done with and through others?

There are a number of distinct leadership benefits that derive from your ability to be present. Here are the benefits that I feel are most important:

Communication Comprehension

- You are better able to "hear" what stakeholders are saying because you are not distracted by your ruminating on other subjects or issues.

Relationship Enhancement

- Your focused attention on the other person assists you in building relationships and strengthening connections.

Managing Risk

- Risk management efforts are more effective, because your greater clarity of thought helps you spot trouble ahead of time.

Your Emotional Welfare

- You will personally feel less stress and anxiety, because you are focusing on what is in front of you now, and you are *not* re-playing past events or worrying about the future.

Having just presented the above list of benefits, I want to now offer two fictional vignettes that help illustrate this often murky concept of *being present.*

The first vignette describes a leader who is *not* being present:

> The team member and the project manager are meeting to talk about a delivery date issue. As the team member speaks, the project manager remains seated behind his desk, frequently glances at his monitor for new emails, and takes a non-urgent phone call. The manager talks over the team member while debating a point, keeps saying, "I know, I know." Periodically, he shuffles papers on his desk, and starts drafting a mental list of what he needs to do tonight to prepare for his flight in the morning.

The second vignette describes a leader who *is* being present:

> When the team member arrives for the meeting, the project manager gets up from behind her desk, moves to a common sitting area, and asks the team member what he'd like to talk about. She makes good eye contact with him, and employs open-ended questions and active listening. During brief periods of silence, she uses the time to "take in" what the team member has just said. Frequently, she checks-in with the team member to ascertain whether the direction of the discussion is helpful to the team member.

Being present, therefore, suggests a series of subtle but powerful messages, delivered to the other person, that cumulatively proclaim:

- I'm here and I am available

- I'm listening, and I am trying to "hear" *your* message

- I want to be of assistance

How Can You Expand Your Leadership Competencies?

Obviously, I have filled the book with my thoughts about how you can develop and enhance your competencies as a leader.

However, in this final chapter, I also want to add a list of assorted other activities that I could engage in (over the next six months, let's say) in order to sharpen my leadership skills. My personal list of activities includes the ideas presented below in Table 12.1:

Table 12.1

Six Months' Worth of Possible Leadership Growth Experiences

Activity or Experience	Details and the Benefit?
Travel, as far as your money will take you, and as often as you can	Foreign travel would be ideal, but if that is not possible, then take yourself to novel urban and rural settings. When you are there, observe the interactions of people. See if you can identify or define any unique ways that people are interacting. Observe one person, and mentally list out all of your beliefs—both positive and negative—that you seem to have for this person.
Spend time where you are "the minority"	Provides chance for you to notice your attributions about the "majority," as well as a chance to consider how "to fit in."
Read something entirely different	Pushes the limits of how you define yourself and your world.
Visualize applying for a job in a foreign country	Requires you to dig deep to find the words that describe your uniqueness and your added value.
Consider hitting the "reset button" on your career	Assists in identifying your desires and goals going forward.
Frequently apply the life-line exercise (presented in Chapter 3) Write down what you would do if you had one year to live	May create a level of discomfort that can propel you forward in making desired changes.
Do one big "stretch" activity, as defined by someone who knows you well	Others can often be better at identifying areas in which you should/can make changes.

Lessons I Have Learned

We all have our lessons learned. Some of these we carry with us in a conscious way (i.e., "Next time I face this problem, I'll never do that again!"), and then there are other lessons that are just as important, but are not often carried with us in obvious ways.

As I think through what I have learned about myself, leadership, and the most beneficial ways to effectively interact with others in a goal directed manner (such as project leadership), I come up with the following list of my lessons learned. Most of these lessons come from my failures.

I Want to Offer "Accurate" Empathy

It is so easy for me to say, "I really understand what you are going through!" when someone is telling me about a big challenge they are facing. Actually, the reality is that I can never *really* know what they are feeling. Therefore, I should refrain from quickly offering such statements, and our discussion would be better served if I focused on:

- Asking open-ended questions
- Using active listening

I Hope to Offer "Incremental" Self-Disclosure

Often, as a means of telling the other person that I really know what they are going through, I can succumb to offering extensive self-disclosure and storytelling, sort of my sharing war stories as a way of letting the person know "that I've been there." Most of the time, the other person does not care about my stories or my difficulties; what they do want is *current* help with their concerns.

So, I need to offer less personal disclosure, and when I do offer it, do so in incremental steps, gauging whether or not it appears to be of any benefit to the other person.

Be a Mensch

I have always liked the word "mensch."

Taken from Yiddish and German, the word, for me, suggests a person of honor and integrity who is a basically "good person." I think of a mensch as someone who treats others well, regardless of one's station in life. Such a person is down to earth, does not put on airs of superiority, and operates in the world in a manner suggestive of the best of being human. A mensch, in my view, sees the common humanity in all people.

Be Present

There are just so many benefits for you, as well as your stakeholders.

Offer What the Other Person Needs, Not Just What I Want To Give Them

I can get excited (often inappropriately so) when I have identified what I think will help a person who is having a difficulty. I may have thought long and hard about the problem, and I may then offer my "solution" with great gusto. And, unfortunately, my good solution may not be what the other person needs (again, just ask my family for confirmation).

So, when a person comes to you with a problem, ask them how you can be of help, rather than adopting my too-frequent approach of giving them *"a great solution."*

Model Authenticity

Whatever you want to see exist within your team culture (positive treatment among team members, a supportive atmosphere, a willingness to actively address conflict, etc.), you first need to demonstrate that approach or attitude in your behavior.

So, your actions need to match your words. You need "to be" what you ask of them "to do."

It's Never Too Late

When working on the interpersonal components of leadership, remember that it is never too late to:

- Make key changes in your own attitudes and behavior
- Address an interpersonal situation that went bad

For example, if you believe that you treated a team member poorly during a meeting, it is never too late to apologize, even if you come to this awareness two weeks after the event.

Some people mistakenly believe that unless a negative interpersonal situation is not made "right" at the time of the event, then it's too late to re-visit it later. Not so. Any gesture you make after such an exchange, even if days after the event, will be productive, and will also serve to enhance the relationship with the team member.

Final Thoughts–For Now

While writing this book, I struggled with trying to capture all of my thoughts on leadership, as well as looking at the published research and commentary on the subject.

I often found myself thinking that I had "covered it all," and then another search would take me in a wildly different direction. At those moments, I felt discouraged and without focus, not knowing when to stop.

However, in observing my process, I came to realize that such a search for all of the information is very similar to one's search to be an excellent leader: there are no "right ways," and the search has no end.

Please see your search towards leadership enhancement as a fluid journey, where you are "OK" where you currently are, and where you can also "be better" down the road.

Always look to identify your current strengths, and then leverage them to develop the additional competencies that you desire. In other words, start with what *is* working, as compared to starting with a focus on what is *not* working.

Be gentle with yourself, as being a leader in the matrix organization of projectized work is an extremely challenging and difficult role. Once again, all the responsibility and none of the authority, as the saying goes.

Enjoy your journey and celebrate your efforts at trying new behaviors. Be present in your dealings with others.

When you are unsure about an interpersonal challenge, ask others for input and support. Paradoxically, you may be delighted to find that the other person will know both more *and* less than you do about leading. Together, you and the other people in your life can support and nudge one another towards leadership growth and fulfillment.

References

Preface

Flannes, S., and Levin, G. (2005). *Essential people skills for project managers.* Vienna, VA: Management Concepts.

Chapter 1: Next Generation Leadership Challenges: What's Coming Your Way

Boyacigiller, N. (2012, March-April). Needed: Executives (and citizens) with a global mindset. *The European Business Review.*

Brown, T. (2009). *Change by design: How design thinking transforms organizations and inspires innovation.* New York: HarperCollins.

Central Intelligence Agency (2013). *The CIA world fact book.* Washington, DC: The Central Intelligence Agency.

Flannes, M. (2011). *Neoliberalism, creative destruction, and the economic reconstruction of Iraq, 2003-2010.* The University of Arizona: Master's Thesis.

Gerush, M., and West, D. (2009). *The PMBOK and Agile: friends or foes?* Cambridge, MA: Forrester Research, Inc.

Holt, K., and Seki, Y. (2012). Global leadership: A developmental shift for everyone. *Industrial and Organizational Psychology*, **5**, 196-215. Washington, DC: Society for Industrial and Organizational Psychology.

PMBOK: A guide to the project management body of knowledge (2008). Newtown Square, PA: Project Management Institute.

Stacey, R. (1996). *Strategic management and organizational dynamics—second edition.* London: Pitman.

Suhonen, M., and Paasivaara, L. (2011). Shared human capital in project management: A systematic review of the literature. *Project Management Journal*, **42**, 4-16.

Chapter 2: Knowing Yourself: There's No Better Place to Start

Cullen, L., and Christopher, T. (2012). Career progression of female accountants in the state public sector. *Australian Accounting Review*, **22**, 68-85.

Flannes, S., and Levin, G. (2005) *Essential people skills for project managers*. Vienna, VA: Management Concepts.

O'Neil, T., and Allen, N. (2010). Personality and the prediction of team performance. *European Journal of Personality*, **25**, 31-42.

Parker, G. (2003). *Cross functional teams: Working with allies, enemies, and other strangers*. San Francisco: Jossey-Bass.

Shapiro, F. (2012). *Getting past your past*. New York: Rodale.

Chapter 3: How to Make Personal Changes

Bugental, J. (1990). *Intimate journeys: Stories from life-changing therapy*. San Francisco: Jossey-Bass.

Flannes, S. (2011). How to maintain high levels of individual and team performance in entrepreneurial and high-paced environments: Applying research-based protocols from the field of resilience. Santa Clara, CA: PMI-Silicon Valley Symposium.

Flannes, S. (2010). Tips for handling the endless stress in project management. Dublin, Ireland: PMI North American Global Congress Proceedings.

Flannes, S., and Levin, G. (2005). *Essential people skills for project managers*. Vienna, VA: Management Concepts.

Chapter 4: Interpersonal Communication Skills for the Global Leader

Ahangar, R. (2012). Emotional intelligence: The most potent factor of job performance among executives. In *Emotional Intelligence: New Perspectives and Applications*, Di Fabio, A. (Ed.). cdn.intechweb.org.

Bharwaney, G., Bar-On, R., and MacKinlay, A. (2011). *EQ and the bottom line: Emotional intelligence increases individual occupational performance, leadership, and organizational change*. Bedfordshire, UK: EiWorld.

Bugental, J. (1990). *Intimate journeys: Stories from life-changing therapy*. San Francisco: Jossey-Bass.

Clarke, N. (2010). Emotional intelligence and its relationship to transformational leadership and key project manager competencies. *Project Management Journal*, **2**, 5-20.

Davis, S. (2011). Investigating the impact of project manager's emotional intelligence on their interpersonal competency. *Project Management Journal*, **42**, 37-57.

Flannes, S., and Levin, G. (2005) *Essential people skills for project managers*. Vienna, VA: Management Concepts.

Goleman, D. (1995). *Emotional intelligence: Why it can matter more than IQ*. New York: Bantam.

Malik, M., Danish, R., and Munir, Y. (2012). The role of transformational leadership and leader's emotional quotient in organizational learning. *World Applied Sciences Journal,* **16**(6), 814-818.

Sigmar, L., Hynes, G., and Hill, K. (2012). Strategies for teaching social and emotional intelligence in business communication. *Business Quarterly Journal,* **75**(3), 2012.

Simic, J., Nesic, L., and Arsenijevic, O. (2012). Emotional intelligence as a stress predictor among managers. *African Journal of Business Management,* **6**(6), 2342-2360.

Tang, H., Yin, M., and Nelson, D. (2010). The relationship between emotional intelligence and leadership practices: A cross-cultural study of academic leaders in Taiwan and the USA. *Journal of Management Psychology,* **8**, 899-926.

Chapter 5: Distinct Leadership Competencies: What You Will Need to Succeed

Dragoni, L., and McAlpine, K. (2012). Leading the business: The criticality of global leaders' cognitive complexity in setting strategic directions. *Industrial and Organizational Psychology* **5**(2), 237-240.

Henderson, L. (2004). Encoding and decoding communication competencies in project management: An exploratory study. *International Journal of Project Management,* **22**, 469-476.

Holt, K., and Seki, Y. (2012). Global leadership: A developmental shift for everyone. *Industrial and Organizational Psychology,* **5**, 196-215.

PMBOK: A guide to the project management body of knowledge (2008). Newtown Square, PA: Project Management Institute.

Probst, G., Raisch, S., and Tushman, M. L. (2011). Ambidextrous leadership: Emerging challenges for business and HR leaders. *Organizational Dynamics* **40**(4), 326-334.

Steers, R.M. et al. (2012). Leadership in a global context: New directions in research and theory development. *Journal of World Business.* doi:10.1016/j.jwb.2012.01.001

Turner, R., and Muller, R. (2005). The project manager's leadership style as a success factor for projects: Literature review. *Project Management Journal,* **36**(2), 49-61.

Youssef, C., and Luthans, F. (2012). Positive global leadership. *Journal of World Business,* **47**, 539-547.

Chapter 6: Achieving and Maintaining High Levels of Performance

American Psychological Association. (2006, March). Multitasking-switching tasks. *The American Psychological Association.* See: www.apa.com.

Begley, S. (2011, March 7). I can't think. *Newsweek.*

Burns, D. (1999). *Feeling good: The new mood therapy.* New York: Harper.

Cornum, R., Mattthews, M., and Seligman, M. (2011). Comprehensive soldier fitness: Building resilience in a challenging institutional context. *American Psychologist,* **66**(1), 4-9.

Csikszentmihalyi, M. (2008). *Flow: The psychology of optimal experience*. New York: Harper Perennial.

Flannes, S. (2013). Stress and project management: Maintaining high performance. A chapter in D. Locke and L. Scott (Eds). *Gower handbook of people in project management*. Farnham, Surrey-U.K.: Gower Publishing Limited.

Flannes, S. (2011). How to maintain high levels of individual and team performance in entrepreneurial and high-paced environments: Applying research-based protocols from the field of resilience. Santa Clara, CA: *PMI- Silicon Valley Chapter Annual Symposium: 2011*.

Flannes, S., and Levin, G. (2005) *Essential people skills for project managers*. Vienna, VA: Management Concepts.

Folke, C. (2010). On resilience: How much disturbance can a system withstand? *SeedMagazine.com*.

Frankl, V. (1958). *Man's search for meaning*. Boston, MA: Beacon Press.

Isett, R., and Isett, B. (2010). *Think right, feel right: The building block guide for happiness and emotional well-being*. See: www.thinkrightfeelright.net.

Kowalski-Trakofler, K., and Vaught, C. (2012). Psycho-social issues in mine emergencies: The impact on the individual, the organization, and the community. *Minerals*, **2**(2), 129-168; doi: 10.3390/min2020129

Nakamura, J., and Csikszentmihalyi, M. (2009). Flow theory and research. In C. Snyder & S. Lopez (Eds), *Handbook for positive psychology*. Oxford: Oxford University Press.

Ng, J., Chan, H., and Schlaghecken, F. (2011, December). Dissociating effects of subclinical anxiety and depression on cognitive control. *Advances in Cognitive Psychology*.

Reich, J., Zautra, A., and Hall, J. (2010). *Handbook of adult resilience*. New York: The Guilford Press.

Rosenman, R,, and Friedman, M. (1977). Modifying Type A behavior pattern. *Journal of Psychosomatic Research*, **21**(4), 323-331.

Rusman, E., van Bruggen, J., Sloep, P., Valcke, M., and Koper, R. (2010). Can I trust you: Personal profiling for a first impression of trustworthiness in virtual project teams. *International Journal of Information Technology Project Management*. (3), 1.

Seligman, M. (2011). *Flourishing: A new visionary understanding of happiness and well-being*. New York: Simon & Shuster, Inc.

Smith, B., Dalen, J., Wiggins, K., Tooley, E., Christopher, P., and Bernard, J. (2008). The brief resilience scale: Assessing the ability to bounce back. *International Journal of Behavioral Medicine*, **15**, 194-200.

Taleb, N. (2007). *The black swan: The impact of the highly improbable*. New York: Random House.

Yerkes, R., and Dodson, J. (1908). The relation of strength of stimulus to rapidity of habituation. *Journal of Comparative Neurology and Psychology*, **18**, 459-480.

Chapter 7: Creating an Effective and Task-Driven Team Culture

Anantatmula, V., and Shrivastav, B. (2012). Evolution of project management teams for Generation Y workforce. *International Journal of Managing Projects in Business*, **5**, 9-26.

Boerner, S., Schaffner, M., and Gebert, D. (2012). The complementarity of team meetings and cross-functional communication: Empirical evidence from new services development teams. *Journal of Leadership and Organizational Studies*, **19**(2), 256-266.

Butler, C., Zander, L., Mockaitis, A., and Sutton, C. (2012). The global leader as boundary spanner, bridge maker, and blender. *Industrial and Organizational Psychology*, **5**(2), 413-431.

DiMarco, M., Taylor, J., and Alin, P. (2009). The emergence and role of cultural boundary spanners in global engineering project networks. *ASCE Journal of Management in Engineering*, **26**(3), 123-132.

Dorairaj, S., Noble, J., and Malik, P. (2012). Distribution and agility: It's all about trust. *Universiti Tenaga National (Malaysia)*, Ph.D. scholarship.

Flannes, S., and Levin, G. (2005) *Essential people skills for project managers*. Vienna, VA: Management Concepts.

Hackman, J., and Wageman, R. (2007, June). Asking the right questions about leadership. *American Psychologist*.

He, J. (2012). Counteracting free-riding with team morale: An experimental study. *Project Management Journal*, **43**(3), 62-75.

O'Neil, T., and Allen, N. (2011). Personality and the prediction of team performance. *European Journal of Personality*, **25**, 31-42.

Peterson, T. (2007). Motivation: How to increase project team performance. *Project Management Journal*, **38**(4), 60-69.

PMBOK: A guide to the project management body of knowledge (2008). Newtown Square, PA: Project Management Institute.

Remidez, H., and Jones, N. (2012). Developing a model for social media in project management communications. *International Journal of Business and Social Science* **3**(3).

Turner, R., Ledwith, A., and Kelly, J. (2010). Project management in small to medium-sized enterprises: Matching processes to the size of the firm. *International Journal of Project Management*, **28**, 744-755.

Woolley, A., Hackman, R., Jerde, T., Chabris, C., Bennet, S., and Kosslyn, S. (2007). Using brain-based measures to compose teams: How individual capabilities and team collaboration strategies jointly shape performance. *Social Neuroscience*, **2**(2), 96-105.

Yeager, K., and Nafukho, F. (2012). Developing diverse teams to improve performance in the organizational setting. *European Journal of Training and Development*, **36**(4), 388-408.

Yeh, J., Wei, C., Wei, C.S., and Lei, D. (2012). The impact of team personality balance on project performance. *African Journal of Business Management*, **6**(4), 1674-1684.

Zander, L. et al. (2012). Leading global teams. *Journal of World Business* . doi:10.1016/j.jwb.2012.01.012.

Zimmerman, A, (2010). Interpersonal relationships in transnational, virtual teams: Towards a configural perspective. *International Journal of Management Reviews*, **13**, 59-78.

Chapter 8: Managing Conflict: Innovative Approaches that Work

Bradley, B., Postlewaite, B., Klotz, A., Hamdani, M., and Brown, K. Reaping the benefits of task conflict in teams: The critical role of team psychological safety climate. *Journal of Applied Psychology*, **97**(1), 151-158.

DiMarco, M., Alin, P., and Taylor, J. (2012). Exploring negotiation through boundary objects in global design project networks. *Project Management Journal*, **43**(3), 24-39.

Farh, J., Lee, C., and Farh, C. (2010). Task conflict and team creativity: A question of how much and when. *Journal of Applied Psychology*, **95**(6), 1173-1180.

Flannes, S., and Levin, G. (2005) *Essential people skills for project managers*. Vienna, VA: Management Concepts.

Killen, D., and Murphy, D. (2003). *Introduction to type and conflict*. Mountain View, CA: Consulting Psychologists Press.

Randeree, K., and El Faramawy, A. (2011). Islamic perspectives on conflict management within project managed environments. *International Journal of Project Management*, **29**, 26-32.

Riaz, M., and Jamal, W. (2012). Horizontal and vertical individualism-collectivism and conflict management styles: A Pakistani sub-cultural model. *Proceedings of the 25th Annual Conference of the International Association for Conflict Management: Cape Town, South Africa.*

Thomas, K. (2005). *Thomas-Kilmann conflict mode instrument*. Mountain View, CA: Consulting Psychologists Press.

Vallacher, P., Coleman, P., Nowak, A., and Bui-Wrzosinska, L. (2010). Rethinking intractable conflict: The perspective of dynamical systems. *American Psychologist*, **65**(4), 262-278.

Chapter 9: Achieving Optimal Productivity & Well-Being in a Fast-Paced Technology Environment: A Win-Win Proposition

Hanson, R. (2009). *Buddha's brain*. Oakland, CA: New Harbinger Publications, Inc.

Chapter 10: Reflections on Leading: My Journey. My Learnings

Jung, C. (2006). *The undiscovered self*. New York: Signet.

Chapter 11: The Gift of Positive Psychology: Fuel for Future Leaders

Csikszentmihalyi, M., and Csikszentmihalyi, I. (Eds.). (1992). *Optimal experience: Psychological studies of flow in consciousness*. Cambridge, UK: Press Syndicate-University of Cambridge.

Csikszentmihalyi, M., and Seligman, M. (2000). Positive psychology: An introduction. *American Psychologist*, **55**(1). See: psycnet.apa.org/psychinfo/2000-13324-001.

Donaldson, S., Dollwet, M., and Rao, M (2014, June). Happiness, excellence, and optimal human functioning revisited: Examining the peer-reviewed literature linked to positive psychology. *The Journal of Positive Psychology*.

Pearce, C. L., and Mihalyi Csikszentmihalyi. (2014). Virtuous leadership revisited: The case of Hüsnü Özyeğin of FIBA Holding. *Journal of Management, Spirituality & Religion*: 1-12.

Reivich, K., Seligman, M., and McBride, S. (2011). Master Resilience Training in the U.S. Army. *American Psychologist,* **66**(1), 25-34.

Seligman, M. (2012). *Flourish: A visionary understanding of happiness and well being.* New York: Free Press/Simon & Schuster.

Chapter 12: Leadership: What Can Your Future Hold?

There are no references cited in this chapter.

Index

www.ingramcontent.com/pod-product-compliance
Lightning Source LLC
Chambersburg PA
CBHW061220220326
41599CB00025B/4697

www.ingramcontent.com/pod-product-compliance
Lightning Source LLC
Chambersburg PA
CBHW061220220326
41599CB00025B/4697